Continental Dishes Made Easy

Susan Graham

HAMLYN
LONDON · NEW YORK · SYDNEY · TORONTO

Contents

First published in the LEISURE-PLAN series
in 1970
by The Hamlyn Publishing Group Limited
London · New York · Sydney · Toronto
Astronaut House, Feltham, Middlesex, England
Second edition published in 1974
© Copyright The Hamlyn Publishing Group
Limited 1974

ISBN 0 600 31822 2

Printed in England by Chapel River Press,
Andover, Hampshire

Acknowledgements
The author and publisher would like to thank the following for their help
and cooperation in supplying colour pictures for this book:

Flour Advisory Bureau: page 49
Fruit Producers' Council: pages 53 and 61
Lard Information Bureau: page 24

Line drawings by Jackie Grippaudo

Useful facts and figures

Metric measures

A convenient method of converting recipe quantities is to round off gramme and millilitre measurements to the nearest unit of 25. The chart below gives the exact conversion (to the nearest whole figure) of Imperial ounces and fluid ounces to grammes and millilitres, and the recommended equivalent based on the nearest unit of 25.

Ounces/fluid ounces	Approx. g. and ml. to nearest whole figure	Recommended conversion to nearest unit of 25
1	28	25
2	57	50
3	85	75
4	113	100
5 ($\frac{1}{4}$ pint)	142	150
6	170	175
7	198	200
8 ($\frac{1}{2}$ lb.)	226	225
9	255	250
10 ($\frac{1}{2}$ pint)	283	275
11	311	300
12	340	350
13	368	375
14	396	400
15 ($\frac{3}{4}$ pint)	428	425
16 (1 lb.)	456	450
17	484	475
18	512	500
19	541	550
20 (1 pint)	569	575

NOTE: When converting quantities over 1 lb. or 1 pint, add together the appropriate figures in the centre column (the direct conversion) before rounding off to the nearest unit of 25.

Throughout the book, we have converted each recipe individually, using the method explained but, where necessary, balancing the proportions of the more critical recipes, such as cakes.

Note on metric units of measurement

1 litre (1000 millilitres, 10 decilitres) equals 1·76 pints, or almost exactly $1\frac{3}{4}$ pints. 1 kilogramme (1000 grammes) equals 2·2 pounds, or almost exactly 2 pounds 3 ounces.

Oven temperature guide

	Electricity		Gas Mark
	°F	°C	
Very cool	225	110	$\frac{1}{4}$
	250	130	$\frac{1}{2}$
Cool	275	140	1
	300	150	2
Moderate	325	170	3
	350	180	4
Moderately hot	375	190	5
	400	200	6
Hot	425	220	7
	450	230	8
Very hot	475	240	9

Notes for American users

Although each recipe has an American measures and ingredients column, the following list gives some American equivalents or substitutes for terms used in the book.

British	American
Deep cake tin	Spring form pan
Frying pan	Skillet
Greaseproof paper	Wax paper
Grill/grilled	Broil/broiled
Kitchen paper	Paper towels
Muslin	Cheesecloth
Patty tins	Muffin pans
Sandwich tin	Layer cake pan
Stoned	Pitted
Swiss roll tin	Jelly roll pan
Mixer/liquidiser	Mixer/blender

NOTE: The British pint is 20 fluid ounces as opposed to the American pint which is 16 fluid ounces.

All cup and spoon measures in this book are level.

Introduction

Holidays abroad, the ease of air travel, television and radio have brought us all much closer together – indeed, the world seems a smaller place as a result.

Foods that used to be sought after and brought back as a special luxury by holidaymakers on the Continent, are now often available in our local supermarkets. The same applies to the special kitchen utensils and serving dishes that were once so hard to track down. Many are today on our doorstep and relatively inexpensive too.

London now boasts a number of Food Centres sponsored by the food producers of a variety of European countries, where one can buy specialised foods and sample national dishes. It is worth spending an hour at one, if you can spare the time when on a trip to London.

Interest in the cooking of other countries has increased tremendously in the past few years. Coupled with this, life for most of us has become busier and fuller.

Much as most of us like to cook, we may have been rather hesitant at trying interesting new dishes for fear that they would be too difficult or take up too much time.

In this book I have endeavoured to include the Continental recipes that are straightforward to make, and to simplify those that are more complicated.

Herbs and spices

We tend to be curiously shy of using herbs and spices in our recipes, which is a great pity. Many of Europe's fortunes were founded on the spice trade, and true Continentals have long known that careful seasoning and flavouring can turn an ordinary recipe into one truly fit for a king. Indeed, the spices we now take for granted were once worth a king's ransom and very highly treasured and sought after.

Much of the food we eat these days is so treated or processed that the flavour is often altered. Enlivened by a few fresh, or well-preserved dried herbs, it will be given a flavour of really natural freshness. It is not a question of camouflaging your cooking, for the art is to use the herbs and spices carefully and with great subtlety to add the mark of success.

A full range of spices is usually available in most stores these days; so too is a range of dried herbs. But if you wish, you can grow your own herbs in the garden, or in a window box, or in flower pots on a window sill.

Here are some hints and suggestions for the use of herbs and spices:

Herbs

Fresh herbs give foods a mild yet distinctive flavour, while the flavour of dried herbs is more concentrated and they should be used sparingly. Therefore only half the suggested amount of fresh herbs will be needed.

Basil Sweet basil is a favourite herb of the Italians, and in Provence. It is first rate in tomato salads and tomato sauces and in salads, soups and stews.

Bay Essential ingredient of bouquet garni. Excellent for flavouring soups and stews.

Chervil Use the leaves in salads, omelettes and as a garnish.

Chives Chives flavour soups, salads and are an ingredient of 'fines herbes' for omelettes. Chopped chives make a good garnish and are an important ingredient for Vichyssoise and Sauce tartare. Add some to cream cheeses for an interesting variation.

Dill Used extensively in Sweden, Russia and Germany where it is eaten with white fish, potatoes and cucumber, besides being used in many hot and cold dishes.

Fennel The leafy portion is used for flavouring fish and sauces, while the seeds add flavour to pastries.

Marjoram Favoured by the Italians. Use it in stuffings, also veal stews.

Mint Flavours sauces and vegetable dishes.

Parsley Used for garnishing, and in sauces, bouquet garni, 'fines herbes' and salad dressings.

Rosemary Good with white meat and fish. Use fresh rosemary in preference to dried.

Sage Best with goose, pork and duck.

Savory – Summer and Winter Use with fish, cheese and egg dishes.

Tarragon Use for salads and soups. Favoured by the French, it is an essential ingredient for Sauce Béarnaise and Sauce verte.

Thyme Always add to a bouquet garni. Good in recipes using wine, in fish soups and stews and with chicken and turkey.

Spices

Be selective and remember to use sparingly. It is as well to bear in mind that spices cannot be kept indefinitely without losing their flavour.

Allspice Rather resembles black peppers in appearance but has a

delicate fragrance. Excellent in meat dishes, sauces and gravies and, carefully used, goes with fruit pies and puddings.

Aniseed The French pound aniseed with sugar to flavour sponges, custards and cream desserts and sprinkle on cakes and biscuits.

Cardamom Ground, it goes well with cakes, pastries and sweet things; it blends well with orange.

Cinnamon Add to fish and fish sauces. Just as good in apple dishes, sweets, sweet sauces and puddings.

Cloves Use cloves whole or ground. They blend well with onion, pork and ham; and are good in sweet dishes, especially gingerbread.

Coriander The Spaniards are fond of using the seeds in bread, cakes and pastries and some meat dishes, while the young leaves go well in sauces and confectionery.

Cumin seeds Use with meat, lamb and chicken. German cooks add cumin to pork and sauerkraut. The Dutch and Swiss like it in cheese.

Ginger Goes well with fruit dishes and sauces.

Mace Use for cakes and sweets; blends well with chocolate; can be used in marinades; add to egg, fish and vegetable dishes. Try it especially with creamed potatoes.

Nutmeg Use as for mace. Ground nutmeg loses its flavour so it is better to keep it whole.

Paprika The Hungarians have practically adopted this spice which originates from Turkey. The Spaniards also favour it.
  A mild pepper which looks attractive sprinkled on egg dishes, fish and cheese dishes and goes ideally with veal or chicken. Not so readily available is a slightly hotter version.

Pepper Black pepper is best ground as it is needed. The white pepper is less pungent and should only be used when specks of black pepper would spoil the appearance of the dish. Cayenne pepper is the hottest pepper and a sparing sprinkle is quite enough to add excitement to a dish!

Turmeric Goes well in chicken, seafood and egg dishes. Also try with rice, creamed potato and macaroni. Mainly noted for the yellow tint it gives to food.

HOW TO MAKE AND USE A BOUQUET GARNI

Herb flavouring can be specially mild if the herbs are tied together or put in a muslin bag and simply suspended in the liquor of the cooking dish. This is known as a bouquet garni and to make one you need:

$\frac{1}{2}$ bay leaf
3–4 stems parsley or 1 level teaspoon dried parsley
1 spray thyme or 1 level teaspoon dried thyme

Tie herbs together in a little bundle or, if dried herbs are used, tie them in muslin and suspend in the dish to be cooked. When the dish is ready to serve, the bouquet garni is removed and thrown away. You can vary the herbs used to suit your taste. For extra speed, use the bought ready-made versions.

First courses

What a problem first courses can be! Thinking up something that will perfectly complement your chosen main course can be more difficult than the rest of the meal put together. There are countless possibilities from abroad, however, for the Continentals have long since learnt to make the very best of available ingredients, and know only too well how to whet the appetite with a delicious introduction to a meal.

The best appetisers are simple and uncomplicated so they fit naturally into this book which is based on easy-to-prepare fare.

Avoid the first course that repeats what is already in the menu. If your main course is a fish dish, its enjoyment would be spoiled should a first course of rollmop herrings have already been eaten. Incidentally, there are many tasty main courses that can be reduced in quantity and served as a first course.

ANTIPASTO
(ITALY)

No cooking

IMPERIAL · METRIC	AMERICAN
anchovy fillets	anchovy fillets
rolled anchovies	rolled anchovies
small mushrooms, cooked in a very little vinegar	small mushrooms, cooked in a very little vinegar
pickled beetroot, cut into tiny shapes	pickled beet, cut into tiny shapes
pickled onions	pickled onions
pimentos	pimientos
sardines	sardines
hard-boiled eggs	hard-cooked eggs
tomatoes, sliced	tomatoes, sliced
olives, green and black	olives, green and ripe

Using as many of these ingredients as you can, arrange them either on individual plates or on one large serving dish, so that the colours form an attractive pattern.

GAMMON SALAD
(SKINKE SALAT – DENMARK)

No cooking

Serves 4

IMPERIAL · METRIC	AMERICAN
1 lb./450 g. cooked gammon	1 lb. cooked cured ham
2 pickled cucumbers	2 dill pickles
$\frac{2}{3}$ pint/4 dl. mayonnaise, seasoned with tarragon vinegar	$1\frac{1}{2}$ cups mayonnaise, seasoned with tarragon vinegar
8 oz./225 g. green peas	$1\frac{1}{2}$ cups green peas
1 head lettuce	1 head lettuce
chervil	chervil

Dice the gammon and the cucumbers. Mix into the mayonnaise with the peas. Make a bed of washed lettuce leaves on a serving dish and place the gammon salad in the centre. Sprinkle with chervil and serve with French bread.

HAM AND MELON
(PROSCIUTTO CON MELONE – ITALY)

No cooking

Serves 5

IMPERIAL · METRIC
2 cantaloupe melons, chilled
8 oz./225 g. Italian cured ham, very
   thinly sliced

AMERICAN
2 cantaloupe melons, chilled
½ lb. Italian cured ham, very thinly
   sliced

Cut each melon into 10 slices and scoop out the seeds. Put slices of the melon on each of five plates and top with the ham.

OPEN SANDWICHES
(SMØRREBRØD – DENMARK)

These open sandwiches can be large or small; there is a huge variety and they are always very colourful and beautifully arranged.

The base can be any kind of bread from rye, pumpernickel or wholemeal, to white bread or crispbread.

Spread generously with butter, or try a pâté, mayonnaise or savoury spread, and top with any of the following:

1 Liver pâté, cold fried bacon, beetroot, cucumber and watercress.
2 Cream cheese, salami or ham, radishes and tomato.
3 Lettuce, rollmops, red cabbage and onion rings.
4 Lettuce, sliced cod roe, sliced onion.
5 Shrimps, hard-boiled egg, parsley and lemon twists.
6 Lettuce, cold roast beef, potato salad and beetroot.
7 Fried eggs, fried tomato and onion rings.
8 Cold roast pork, aspic jelly and pickled prunes.
9 Sliced cheese, celery and tomato.
10 Hot fried filleted plaice, tartare sauce, parsley and lemon.

These are just suggestions – there are many, many more versions. Incidentally, eat Smørrebrød with a knife and fork.

COLD BUFFET TABLE
(SMORGÅSBORD AND KOLDTBORD – SCANDINAVIA)

Delicious cold savouries, breads and salads served as either a first course or as a main meal.

Ideas for cold buffet tables
Potted shrimps, jellied eels, sliced cold meats, egg mayonnaise, rollmops, sardines, salmon in various forms, liver sausage and salami, hard-boiled eggs and various salads. Also:

Pickled herrings
Cut fillets of fresh herring in pieces. Slice onions. Fill a pie dish with herrings and onions, half fill with vinegar, add peppercorns, 1 teaspoon sugar and bay leaf. Cover and keep in liquor. Serve cold.

Herring salad
Mix diced beetroot, sour apple, chopped pickled herring, chopped onion with mayonnaise.

Swedish salad
Mix potato salad with chopped raw kipper or smoked salmon, onion and pickled cucumber.

Herring mayonnaise
Steam fresh herring in a steamer for 10 minutes and allow to get cold. Make a creamy mayonnaise by mixing evaporated milk, curry powder and lemon juice with bottled or home-made salad cream. Mix the mayonnaise and herring together before serving.

ROLLMOP HERRINGS ON A SAVOURY BASE

(HARING KAASSLA – HOLLAND)

No cooking

Serves 6

IMPERIAL · METRIC	AMERICAN
6 oz./175 g. Gouda cheese	6 oz. Gouda cheese
1 apple	1 apple
6 celery sticks	6 celery stalks
6 gherkins	6 sweet dill pickles
6 oz./175 g. cooked peas	1 generous cup cooked peas
1 small packet mixed frozen vegetables, cooked	1 small package mixed frozen vegetables, cooked
salt and pepper	salt and pepper
mayonnaise (see page 75)	mayonnaise (see page 75)
6 rollmop herrings	6 rollmop herring
grapes and parsley to garnish	grapes and parsley to garnish

Cut the cheese, apple, celery and gherkins into small cubes. Mix with the peas, mixed vegetables and seasoning. Blend with a little mayonnaise and pile into a dish. Arrange rollmops over the top and garnish with halved, stoned grapes and parsley.

MUSSELS IN WINE

(MOULES À LA MARINIÈRE – FRANCE)

Cooking time: 10 minutes

Serves 8

IMPERIAL · METRIC	AMERICAN
4 pints/2¼ litres mussels	5 pints mussels
2 onions, finely chopped	2 onions, finely chopped
½ pint/3 dl. dry white wine	1¼ cups dry white wine
bouquet garni	bouquet garni
shake pepper	shake pepper
2 oz./50 g. butter	¼ cup butter
chopped parsley to garnish	chopped parsley to garnish

Wash and scrub the mussels thoroughly in cold water. Remove the beard and any foreign bodies attached to the shells, using a sharp knife. Rinse in a bowl of fresh water, stir and drain in a colander.

Put the mussels into a large pan with the onions, wine and bouquet garni. Season with pepper. Simmer gently for about 5 minutes until the mussels open up. Remove the bouquet garni and any unopened mussels and discard. Drain the rest of the mussels, reserving the cooking liquor. Retain only the halves of the shells to which the mussels are attached and place them on a hot serving plate. Reheat the reserved liquor, stir in the butter and strain over mussels. Sprinkle with parsley.

FISH ROE PÂTÉ

(TARAMASALATA – GREECE)

No cooking

Serves 6

IMPERIAL · METRIC	AMERICAN
8 oz./225 g. white bread, soaked in water and drained thoroughly	½ lb. white bread, soaked in water and drained thoroughly
8 oz./225 g. smoked fish roe	1 cup smoked fish roe
little finely chopped onion	little finely chopped onion
juice of 1½ lemons	juice of 1½ lemons
⅓ pint/2½ dl. salad oil	generous ¾ cup salad oil

Put the bread, roe, onion and lemon juice in a liquidiser at a slow speed and add the oil gradually until a smooth paste. Serve with olives and cucumber.

COCKTAIL BITS
(BITTERBALLEN – HOLLAND)

Cooking time: 10 minutes

Makes 30–40

IMPERIAL · METRIC	AMERICAN
¼ oz./10 g. gelatine	1 envelope gelatin
½ pint/3 dl. stock	1¼ cups stock
1 oz./25 g. butter	2 tablespoons butter
1 oz./25 g. plain flour	¼ cup all-purpose flour
6 oz./175 g. cooked ham and veal, chopped	¾ cup cooked chopped ham and veal
1 oz./25 g. Gouda cheese, grated	¼ cup grated Gouda cheese
1 teaspoon chopped parsley	1 teaspoon chopped parsley
seasoning	seasoning
3 oz./75 g. toasted breadcrumbs	¾ cup toasted bread crumbs
1 small egg	1 egg
fat for deep frying	oil for deep frying

Add the gelatine to the stock, heating gently until thoroughly dissolved. Melt the butter, add flour, cook for 5 minutes and then beat in the stock. Cook until thickened. Add the meat, cheese and parsley. Season well. Turn on to a plate and allow to cool until firm. Roll into small balls, dip into breadcrumbs, then into beaten egg and lastly into breadcrumbs again. Fry in hot fat until golden brown and then drain on absorbent paper. Serve with mild mustard.

STUFFED EGGS
(OEUFS FARCIS – FRANCE)

Cooking time: 15 minutes

Serves 4

IMPERIAL · METRIC	AMERICAN
2 eggs	2 eggs
4 slices brown bread, buttered	4 slices brown bread, buttered
4 tablespoons cottage cheese	5 tablespoons cottage cheese
paprika pepper	paprika pepper

Hard-boil the eggs, shell and cut in half, lengthwise. Remove the yolks and sieve on to a plate. Cut the crusts off the bread and put half an egg white on each slice. Blend the egg yolk and cottage cheese. Fill each egg white with this mixture. Sprinkle with paprika pepper.

GRAPEFRUIT AND GINGER
(PAMPLEMOUSSE AU GINGEMBRE – FRANCE)

No cooking

Serves 4

IMPERIAL · METRIC	AMERICAN
2 grapefruit, cut in half	2 grapefruit, cut in half
2 tablespoons sherry	3 tablespoons sherry
1 oz./25 g. sugar	2 tablespoons sugar
½ teaspoon grated nutmeg	½ teaspoon grated nutmeg
½ teaspoon ground ginger	½ teaspoon ground ginger
1 oz./25 g. preserved ginger	few pieces preserved ginger
4 glacé cherries	4 candied cherries

Prepare the grapefruit by dividing them into sections with a knife. Sprinkle over the sherry, sugar, nutmeg and ground ginger. Chop the preserved ginger into small pieces and scatter over the grapefruit. Top with glacé cherries. Allow to stand for about 1 hour before serving.

Soups

Many Continental countries start their midday meal with a good soup. These are served with scores of different garnishes – noodles, poached eggs, squares of pasta, rice, gnocchi, shredded pancakes, to name but a few.

Even if you are devoted to your can opener when it comes to soups, you can liven them up with interesting garnishes. We have much to learn here from our friends across the Channel. The garnish makes the soup course much more appetising and, because it makes it more substantial, it can become a meal in itself.

FISH SOUP
(BOUILLABAISSE – FRANCE)
Illustrated in colour on page 20

Cooking time: 35 minutes

Serves 6

IMPERIAL · METRIC	AMERICAN
2 lb./1 kg. fish made up from: trout, conger eel, rock salmon, gurnard, plaice or turbot, lobster, crab, prawns and mussels	2 lb. fish made up from: red snapper, halibut, pompano, sea perch, scallops, lobster, shrimp, clams and mussels
2 onions	2 onions
2 leeks	2 leeks
$\frac{1}{4}$ pint/1$\frac{1}{2}$ dl. olive oil	$\frac{2}{3}$ cup olive oil
$\frac{1}{4}$ pint/1$\frac{1}{2}$ dl. dry white wine	$\frac{2}{3}$ cup dry white wine
2 pints/generous 1 litre fish stock	5 cups fish stock
4 oz./100 g. tomatoes, skinned, seeded and roughly chopped	$\frac{1}{4}$ lb. tomatoes, skinned, seeded and roughly chopped
2 cloves garlic, crushed	2 cloves garlic, crushed
bouquet garni	bouquet garni
salt and pepper	salt and pepper
$\frac{1}{2}$ teaspoon powdered saffron	$\frac{1}{2}$ teaspoon powdered saffron
2 level tablespoons arrowroot	3 level tablespoons arrowroot flour
4 tablespoons cold water	5 tablespoons cold water
2 oz./50 g. butter	$\frac{1}{4}$ cup butter
1 small French loaf	1 small French loaf
sprigs of parsley to garnish	sprigs of parsley to garnish

Cut off fish heads, tails and fins. Wash and clean the fish, cut into large pieces and put into a large size saucepan. Clean and cut up the shellfish, where necessary, and set aside. Skin and chop the onions, wash the leeks and chop white parts.

Heat the oil in a large pan and sauté the onions and leeks until tender, without allowing them to brown. Add the wine and stock, the tomatoes, 1 clove of garlic and the bouquet garni. Season with salt and pepper and add the saffron. Add to the fish; bring to the boil and simmer for 15 minutes. Remove the fish to a dish. Add the shellfish to the pan until just heated, then remove from the pan and add to the fish.

Strain the liquid through a fine sieve into a clean pan and bring to the boil. Adjust seasoning. Blend the arrowroot with the cold water, add to the liquid in the pan, return to the heat and cook briskly for 5 minutes, uncovered. At the last moment add half the butter.

Spread some thin slices of French bread with the rest of the butter flavoured with the remaining clove of garlic, and grill. Replace the fish in the liquid in the pan. Allow to reheat. Spoon the fish into a serving dish, pour on the liquid and scatter with the bread. Garnish with parsley.

MUSHROOM SOUP

(CRÈME DE CHAMPIGNONS –
FRANCE)

Cooking time: 40 minutes

Serves 4

IMPERIAL · METRIC	AMERICAN
8 oz./225 g. mushrooms	2 cups mushrooms
1 small onion	1 small onion
½ pint/3 dl. stock	1¼ cups stock
2 oz./50 g. butter	¼ cup butter
1 oz./25 g. flour	¼ cup all-purpose flour
1 pint/6 dl. milk	2½ cups milk
salt and pepper	salt and pepper

Chop the mushrooms, reserving a few whole ones for garnish. Skin and chop the onion. Put the chopped mushrooms and onion in a pan with the stock and bring to the boil. Cover and simmer slowly until tender. Rub the mixture through a sieve.

Melt half the butter in a pan and stir in the flour. Allow to cook over gentle heat for 1 minute. Stir in the milk gradually and continue stirring until the mixture thickens and boils. Stir in the mushroom purée and season well with salt and pepper. Simmer gently for 15 minutes.

Meanwhile slice the reserved whole mushrooms and sauté in the remaining butter until tender. Serve the soup piping hot, garnished with the sautéed mushrooms.

POTATO SOUP

(SOPA DE PATATAS – SPAIN)

Cooking time: 30 minutes

Serves 6–8

IMPERIAL · METRIC	AMERICAN
2 medium onions, chopped	2 medium onions, chopped
2 tablespoons olive oil	3 tablespoons olive oil
¼ teaspoon salt	¼ teaspoon salt
2 tablespoons dry sherry	3 tablespoons dry sherry
2½ pints/1¼ litres chicken stock (made from stock cubes)	6¼ cups chicken stock (made from bouillon cubes)
6 potatoes, peeled and diced	6 potatoes, peeled and diced
sprigs mint or 2 tablespoons chopped parsley	sprigs mint or 3 tablespoons chopped parsley

Cook the onions slowly in olive oil until very tender, sprinkling with salt as they cook; add the sherry and stock. Bring to the boil, add the raw potatoes and cook until tender. Before serving, mash the potatoes in the stock and garnish with sprigs of mint or parsley.

PEA SOUP

(ERWTENSOEP – HOLLAND)

Cooking time: 2 hours 20 minutes

Serves 4–6

IMPERIAL · METRIC	AMERICAN
1 lb./½ kg. dried split peas	1 lb. dried split peas
1-lb./½-kg. piece boiling bacon	1-lb. piece boiling ham
1 marrow bone	1 marrow bone
1 lb./½ kg. potatoes	1 lb. potatoes
1 pint/6 dl. milk	2½ cups milk
salt and pepper	salt and pepper
½ head celery	½ bunch celery
1 lb./½ kg. leeks	1 lb. leeks
½ tablespoon chopped parsley	½ tablespoon chopped parsley

Wash the peas and soak overnight in 3 pints (1½ litres, 7½ cups) water.

Simmer the meat and bone for 1 hour in 3 pints (1½ litres, 7½ cups) boiling water. Add the peas and the water they soaked in. Simmer for 20 minutes, then add the sliced potatoes. Simmer for a further 40 minutes. Remove the bacon and marrow bone. Scoop out the marrow and return to the soup. Sieve the soup and add the milk. Season well and add the diced celery and leek. Simmer for 20 minutes. Add parsley and serve hot.

COLD SUMMER SOUP
(GAZPACHO – SPAIN)

No cooking

Serves 4

IMPERIAL · METRIC	AMERICAN
1½ oz./40 g. breadcrumbs	¾ cup bread crumbs
2 tablespoons red wine vinegar	3 tablespoons red wine vinegar
2 cloves garlic	2 cloves garlic
salt and pepper	salt and pepper
1 medium cucumber, peeled	1 medium cucumber, peeled
1 small green pepper, seeded	1 small green sweet pepper, seeded
1 onion	1 onion
4 tablespoons salad oil	⅓ cup salad oil
2 lb./1 kg. tomatoes, skinned	2 lb. tomatoes, skinned
¼ pint/1½ dl. iced water	⅔ cup iced water
croûtons to serve	croûtons to serve

Put the breadcrumbs in a bowl with the vinegar and leave for 10 minutes. Crush the garlic with a teaspoon of salt. Finely chop most of the cucumber, coarsely chop half the green pepper, skin and chop the onion. Mix together the breadcrumbs, garlic, chopped cucumber, green pepper and onion. Blend to a paste in a liquidiser or turn into a bowl and pound with a pestle, or mince twice. Stir in the oil, a few drops at a time. Rub the tomatoes through a sieve and add to the mixture with the iced water. Season and chill well. Chop finely the rest of the cucumber and green pepper and add to the soup. Serve well chilled and hand round croûtons.

LENTIL SOUP
(SOPA DE LENTEJAS MADRILEÑA – SPAIN)

Cooking time: 2 hours 10 minutes

Serves 6–8

IMPERIAL · METRIC	AMERICAN
1 large onion, chopped	1 large onion, chopped
1 green pepper, seeded and diced	1 green sweet pepper, seeded and diced
1 canned red pepper (pimento), drained and diced	1 canned red pepper (pimiento), drained and diced
4 tablespoons olive oil	⅓ cup olive oil
2 tablespoons flour	3 tablespoons all-purpose flour
1 large can tomatoes	1 large can tomatoes
4 carrots, scraped and diced	4 carrots, cleaned and diced
1 tablespoon salt	1 tablespoon salt
1 lb./½ kg. lentils, unsoaked	1 lb. lentils, unsoaked
3 pints/1½ litres water	7½ cups water

Simmer the onion, green pepper and canned red pepper in the olive oil until very soft. Stir in the flour, cook until bubbling but do not brown. Add the tomatoes, carrots, salt, lentils and water. Simmer covered, over very low heat for 2–3 hours, stirring occasionally.

COLD BEETROOT SOUP

(BORTSCH – RUSSIA)

Cooking time: 1 hour 20 minutes

Serves 6

IMPERIAL · METRIC	AMERICAN
2 large raw beetroots	2 large raw beets
2 onions	2 onions
2 leeks	2 leeks
$\frac{1}{4}$ cabbage	$\frac{1}{4}$ cabbage
3 oz./75 g. butter	6 tablespoons butter
4 oz./100 g. tomatoes	$\frac{1}{4}$ lb. tomatoes
3 tablespoons cider vinegar	scant $\frac{1}{4}$ cup cider vinegar
3 pints/1$\frac{1}{2}$ litres chicken or beef stock	7$\frac{1}{2}$ cups chicken or beef stock
1 tablespoon sugar	1 tablespoon sugar
1–2 bay leaves	1–2 bay leaves
sprig parsley	sprig parsley
salt and pepper	salt and pepper
soured cream, sliced ham or frankfurter sausages to serve	sour cream, sliced cured ham or frankfurter sausages to serve

Wash, peel and finely shred the beetroots. Skin and chop the onions. Clean and chop the leeks and shred the cabbage. Heat the butter in a heavy pan and add all the vegetables. Cook very slowly for 20 minutes. Add the vinegar, stock, sugar and seasonings and bring to the boil. Adjust the seasoning and simmer for 1 hour. Serve cold with soured cream, and sliced ham or frankfurter sausages.

FRENCH ONION SOUP

(SOUPE À L'OIGNON – FRANCE)

Cooking time: 2 hours 10 minutes
Oven temperature: 350°F., 180°C., Gas Mark 4

Serves 4–6

IMPERIAL · METRIC	AMERICAN
2 oz./50 g. butter	$\frac{1}{4}$ cup butter
1 tablespoon olive oil	1 tablespoon olive oil
4 onions	4 onions
1 head celery	1 bunch celery
1 bay leaf	1 bay leaf
1 teaspoon salt	1 teaspoon salt
1 teaspoon black peppercorns	1 teaspoon black peppercorns
3 pints/1$\frac{1}{2}$ litres boiling water	7$\frac{1}{2}$ cups boiling water
1 small French loaf	1 small French loaf
8 oz./225 g. Cheddar cheese	$\frac{1}{2}$ lb. Cheddar cheese

Melt the butter and oil in a large saucepan. Skin and slice the onions, add to the saucepan and cook very gently until tender but not browned. Wash the celery very thoroughly and slice both leaves and stalks into pieces. Add to the onions with the bay leaf, salt and peppercorns. Mix all together well, cover with a well-fitting lid and leave to simmer for 5 minutes. Pour in the boiling water. Cover and leave to simmer for 1 hour.
  Slice the loaf of bread thinly and cover the bottom of an ovenproof casserole. Sprinkle with cheese. Build up the casserole with layers of cheese and bread until the dish is well over half full. Strain over the onion and celery mixture until the dish is full. Cover and cook for 1 hour in the centre of a moderately hot oven. Serve piping hot.

VICHYSSOISE
(FRANCE)

Cooking time: 10 minutes

Serves 4

IMPERIAL · METRIC	AMERICAN
1½ oz./40 g. butter	3 tablespoons butter
2 leeks, sliced	2 leeks, sliced
1 small onion, chopped	1 small onion, chopped
1 stick celery, chopped	1 stalk celery, chopped
1 large potato, peeled and sliced	1 large potato, peeled and sliced
sprig parsley	sprig parsley
2 drops Worcestershire sauce	2 drops Worcestershire sauce
1 pint/6 dl. white stock	2½ cups white stock
salt and pepper	salt and pepper
½ pint/3 dl. single cream	1¼ cups coffee cream
chopped chives to garnish	chopped chives to garnish

Melt the butter in a pan, add the leeks and onion. Cook gently until tender. Add the celery and potato, cook for a minute or two and then stir in the parsley, Worcestershire sauce and stock. Season well.
 Put half the mixture into a liquidiser and blend for 1 minute, or pass it through a sieve. Repeat with the remainder. Chill until ready to serve. Stir in the cream and serve topped with a few chopped chives.

VEGETABLE SOUP
(GRÖNSAKSSOPPA – SWEDEN)

Cooking time: 30 minutes

Serves 4

IMPERIAL · METRIC	AMERICAN
1 small head cauliflower, divided into florets	1 small head cauliflower, divided into florets
5 oz./150 g. fresh or frozen peas	scant 1 cup fresh or frozen peas
4 small carrots, sliced	4 small carrots, sliced
1¼ pints/¾ litre salted water	3 cups salted water
1 pint/6 dl. milk	2½ cups milk
2½ oz./65 g. flour	generous ½ cup all-purpose flour
salt and pepper	salt and pepper

Cook the vegetables in the salted water until nearly tender. Blend the milk and flour and whisk into the soup. Simmer for 5 minutes, stirring occasionally. Season. Serve hot with cheese and hard biscuits, rusks or crackers.

BEER AND MILK SOUP
(BIERSUPPE MIT MILCH – GERMANY)

Cooking time: 10 minutes

Serves 6

IMPERIAL · METRIC	AMERICAN
2 pints/generous 1 litre beer	5 cups beer
juice of ½ lemon	juice of ½ lemon
piece cinnamon stick	piece cinnamon stick
1 pint/6 dl. milk	2½ cups milk
2 egg yolks	2 egg yolks
sugar	sugar
salt	salt

Heat the beer in a pan with the lemon juice and cinnamon. Heat the milk and pour it over the egg yolks, whisking. Add to the hot beer and season with sugar and salt.

COD WITH MIXED VEGETABLES

(TORSK MED BLANDEDE GRØNNSAKER – NORWAY)

Cooking time: 15 minutes

Serves 3–4

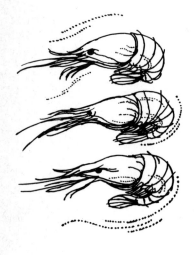

IMPERIAL · METRIC	AMERICAN
1 large packet frozen cod fillets	1 large package frozen cod fillets
about ½ pint/3 dl. milk	about 1¼ cups milk
salt and pepper	salt and pepper
2 tablespoons chopped parsley	3 tablespoons chopped parsley
1 small packet frozen mixed vegetables	1 small package frozen mixed vegetables
1 oz./25 g. butter	2 tablespoons butter
1 oz./25 g. flour	¼ cup all-purpose flour
2 teaspoons lemon juice	2 teaspoons lemon juice
1 small packet frozen prawns	1 small package frozen prawns or shrimp

Cut the cod fillets into small pieces. Place in a pan with the milk, seasonings and parsley. Bring to the boil, reduce heat and simmer for 12–15 minutes. Remove the fish carefully and keep hot.

Add the mixed vegetables to the milk that the cod was cooked in and bring back to the boil. Simmer and cook for 8–10 minutes. Strain and add the vegetables to the fish; keep hot.

Make the liquor up to ½ pint (3 dl., 1¼ cups) again by adding more milk. Work the butter and flour into a ball, whisk into the milk and bring to the boil. Reduce the heat and cook for a further 3–4 minutes. Stir in the lemon juice and season to taste. Pour over the fish and vegetables; add some of the defrosted prawns.

Garnish with the remaining prawns and serve hot.

MEAT DUMPLINGS IN SOUP

(YOUVARLAKIA – GREECE)

Cooking time: 45 minutes

Serves 4

IMPERIAL · METRIC	AMERICAN
1 lb./½ kg. minced beef	1 lb. ground beef
1 onion, chopped	1 onion, chopped
1 clove garlic, crushed	1 clove garlic, crushed
salt and pepper	salt and pepper
1 teaspoon chopped parsley	1 teaspoon chopped parsley
3 oz./75 g. long grain rice, cooked	scant ½ cup long grain rice, cooked
1 egg	1 egg
1 oz./25 g. flour	¼ cup all-purpose flour
2 pints/generous 1 litre water	5 cups water
1 (8-oz./225-g.) can tomatoes	1 (8-oz.) can tomatoes
2 egg yolks	2 egg yolks
juice of 1 lemon	juice of 1 lemon

Mix the meat, onion, garlic, salt, pepper, parsley and half of the rice. Bind with the egg and form into balls. Roll in flour. Boil the water with the canned tomato, season well. Add the rest of the rice and meat balls, cover and simmer for 30 minutes. Beat the 2 egg yolks with a little water and the lemon juice. Add to the soup, but do not allow it to boil. Serve at once.

Fish dishes

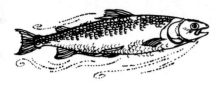

Why, oh why do we make so little of our fish? Many of us think only of frying it. The Continentals are much more clever. They poach fish in wine, stuff, bake or grill it, and make pâtés; with the fish usually goes the most delicious sauce to complement it. All these methods are so easy, so appetising and rarely take very long.

It isn't always possible to use the traditional fish for such superb dishes as Bouillabaisse, because they are simply strangers to our shores. However, it is easy to substitute a fish that is available here, with very little change to the final flavour of the dish.

GARLIC SAUCE WITH COD AND VEGETABLES
(AÏOLI – FRANCE)

Cooking time: 20–30 minutes

Serves 4

IMPERIAL · METRIC
4–7 cloves garlic, peeled and
   crushed
2 egg yolks
½ pint/3 dl. olive oil
2 teaspoons lemon juice, strained
portions of: globe artichokes,
   courgettes, new potatoes, young
   carrots, Jerusalem artichokes,
   French beans, cauliflower florets

4 cod fillets

AMERICAN
4–7 cloves garlic, peeled and
   crushed
2 egg yolks
1¼ cups olive oil
2 teaspoons lemon juice, strained
portions of: globe artichokes,
   small zucchini, new potatoes,
   young carrots, Jerusalem
   artichokes, green beans,
   cauliflower florets

4 cod fillets

Crush the cloves of garlic in a basin. Add the egg yolks and stir well. Drip in the oil, beating well until the mixture thickens. Add the lemon juice. Cook the vegetables by steaming them. Steam the fillets. To serve, arrange everything decoratively on a large platter with the aïoli in the centre.

PRAWN SOUFFLÉ
(REKESUFFLE – NORWAY)

Cooking time: 20 minutes
Oven temperature: 425°F., 220°C.,
Gas Mark 7

Serves 2

IMPERIAL · METRIC
2 eggs, separated
1 tablespoon grated cheese
1 small packet frozen prawns,
   defrosted
salt and pepper
butter
Sherry sauce:
2 egg yolks
1 tablespoon sweet sherry

AMERICAN
2 eggs, separated
1 tablespoon grated cheese
1 small package frozen prawns or
   shrimp, defrosted
salt and pepper
butter
Sherry sauce:
2 egg yolks
1 tablespoon sweet sherry

Whisk the egg whites stiffly. In another bowl, combine the egg yolks, cheese, defrosted prawns and seasoning. Stir in the egg whites carefully. Melt a little butter in a soufflé dish. Pile the mixture into the dish and bake in a hot oven for 20 minutes. Serve the soufflé at once with the sherry sauce.

To make the sherry sauce, beat the egg yolks and sherry over hot water until light and fluffy.

Alternatively a tomato sauce (see pages 52 or 77) may be used.

SMOKED HADDOCK WITH LEMON CREAM SPINACH

(ROKET KOLJE MED SITRON OG SPINATSTUING – NORWAY)

Cooking time: 15 minutes

Serves 3–4

IMPERIAL · METRIC	AMERICAN
1 large packet frozen smoked haddock	1 large package frozen smoked haddock
1 large packet frozen creamed spinach	1 large package frozen creamed spinach
2 tablespoons soured cream	3 tablespoons sour cream
$\frac{1}{2}$ tablespoon lemon juice	$\frac{1}{4}$ tablespoon lemon juice
pinch salt	pinch salt
black pepper	black pepper
lemon butterflies and tomato slices to garnish	lemon butterflies and tomato slices to garnish

Defrost the smoked haddock sufficiently to separate the fillets, poach in a shallow pan for 15 minutes. Prepare the spinach in a pan according to packet instructions. Add the soured cream, lemon juice, salt and pepper. Remove the skin from the fish and flake with a fork. Place in a serving dish and cover with the spinach. Garnish with lemon butterflies and tomato slices.

BAKED HERRINGS

(HARENG AU FOUR – FRANCE)

Cooking time: 45 minutes
Oven temperature: 375° F., 190° C., Gas Mark 5

Serves 4

IMPERIAL · METRIC	AMERICAN
4 herrings	4 herring
salt	salt
ground black pepper	ground black pepper
2 small onions	2 small onions
1 oz./25 g. butter, melted	2 tablespoons melted butter
1 lb./$\frac{1}{2}$ kg. tomatoes	1 lb. tomatoes
1 teaspoon sugar	1 teaspoon sugar
2 tablespoons vinegar	3 tablespoons vinegar
1 teaspoon roughly chopped parsley	1 teaspoon roughly chopped parsley

Well grease an ovenproof dish. Clean the herrings, removing heads and trimming fins and tails. Make light slashes on each side of the fish and season well. Peel the onions and slice into thin wedges. Lightly fry in half the quantity of butter for 5 minutes. Plunge the tomatoes in boiling water for a moment, then remove skins and cut into wedges. Make a bed of tomato and fried onion wedges on the bottom of the dish. Sprinkle with sugar, salt, plenty of black pepper and vinegar. Arrange the herrings on top and brush with melted butter. Cover with foil or a lid and bake in a moderately hot oven for 45 minutes. Serve piping hot, sprinkled with chopped parsley.

SOLE IN BUTTER

(SOLE MEUNIÈRE – FRANCE)

Fry frozen fillets of sole in melted butter until the flesh parts easily when tested with a knife. Serve with a little extra butter poured over them, and garnish with chopped parsley and slices of lemon.

SOLE WITH ORANGE SAUCE

(LENGUADO CON SALSA DE NARANJAS – SPAIN)

Cooking time: 20 minutes

Serves 4

IMPERIAL · METRIC	AMERICAN
2 lb./1 kg. filleted sole	2 lb. filleted sole
2 tablespoons olive oil	3 tablespoons olive oil
$\frac{1}{2}$ oz./15 g. butter	1 tablespoon butter
3 tablespoons chopped onion	$\frac{1}{4}$ cup chopped onion
$\frac{1}{2}$ pint/3 dl. canned orange juice	$1\frac{1}{4}$ cups canned orange juice
1 teaspoon grated orange rind	1 teaspoon grated orange rind
4 tablespoons dry white wine	$\frac{1}{3}$ cup dry white wine
$\frac{3}{4}$ teaspoon salt	$\frac{3}{4}$ teaspoon salt

Fry the fish in olive oil and butter until golden on one side, turn and add the onion to the pan. Cook over a moderate heat until the onion is tender. Remove the fish and keep hot. Add the remaining ingredients to the pan and simmer for 10 minutes. Return the fish to the sauce. Cook for 5–10 minutes longer until the fish flakes easily.

RECIPES FOR MUSSELS

(RECETTES POUR MOULES – BELGIUM)

Choose heavy, tightly closed mussels. Before cooking, wash well several times and scrape them. To open, put them in a pan, without water, on a low heat and as they warm the shells will open. Discard any that don't open.

Moules à l'escargot

Open mussels and leave on the half shell. Mix 3 oz. (75 g., 6 tablespoons) butter, 2 crushed or finely chopped cloves of garlic, a little chopped parsley, pepper and salt. Put a piece of this savoury butter, the size of a large pea, on each mussel, arrange in a shallow ovenproof dish and cook in a moderate oven for 5 minutes. Serve hot with a squeeze of lemon juice.

Moules au gratin

Allow 4 pints ($2\frac{1}{4}$ litres, 5 pints) mussels for 6 people. Clean and scrape them and put in a casserole with a chopped onion, a bay leaf, thyme and parsley. Cook for about 5 minutes. Take out and remove from the shells. Place the mussels in a fireproof dish and cover with a few thinly sliced cooked mushrooms. On top, spread a thick, well-seasoned white sauce made with half milk and half mussel liquor (see page 76). Dot with butter and sprinkle with brown breadcrumbs and grated cheese. Brown under a hot grill.

Moules à la provençale

Put shelled, cooked mussels in an ovenproof dish and add tomato sauce (see page 52 or 77) flavoured with crushed garlic and finely chopped anchovies. Cook slowly until the mussels are cooked through.

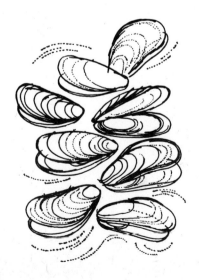

Bouillabaisse (page 11)

FISH CASSEROLE

(KALALAATIKKO – FINLAND)

Cooking time: 50 minutes
Oven temperature: 350°F., 180°C.,
Gas Mark 4

Serves 6

IMPERIAL · METRIC	AMERICAN
1 lb./$\frac{1}{2}$ kg. fish fillets	1 lb. fish fillets
6 medium potatoes, sliced	6 medium potatoes, sliced
2 carrots, sliced	2 carrots, sliced
1 onion, chopped	1 onion, chopped
1 bay leaf	1 bay leaf
salt	salt
$\frac{3}{4}$ pint/4 dl. milk	scant 2 cups milk
1 egg	1 egg
1 tablespoon breadcrumbs	1 tablespoon bread crumbs
1 oz./25 g. butter	2 tablespoons butter

Cut the fish into pieces. Layer the fish, potatoes and other vegetables in a buttered baking dish. Add the bay leaf and salt. Mix the milk and egg and pour over the casserole to barely cover it. Sprinkle with breadcrumbs and dot with the butter.

  Bake in a moderate oven, until the vegetables and potatoes are tender – about 50 minutes. Serve hot from the dish.

SOLE BAKED IN SOURED CREAM

(SOLA ZAPIEKANA – POLAND)

Cooking time: 20 minutes
Oven temperature: 400°F., 200°C.,
Gas Mark 6

Serves 6–7

IMPERIAL · METRIC	AMERICAN
2 lb./1 kg. sole	2 lb. sole
salt and pepper	salt and pepper
1 oz./25 g. flour	$\frac{1}{4}$ cup all-purpose flour
2 oz./50 g. butter	$\frac{1}{4}$ cup butter
4 tablespoons grated Parmesan	5 tablespoons grated Parmesan
$\frac{1}{4}$ pint/1$\frac{1}{2}$ dl. soured cream	$\frac{2}{3}$ cup sour cream
$\frac{1}{2}$ tablespoon flour	$\frac{1}{2}$ tablespoon all-purpose flour
breadcrumbs and butter for topping	bread crumbs and butter for topping
lemon slices	lemon slices

Season the fish and dust with flour. Brown lightly in the butter. Arrange in a shallow baking dish. Sprinkle thickly with Parmesan. Pour in the soured cream, to which $\frac{1}{2}$ tablespoon flour has been added. Sprinkle with breadcrumbs and top with pieces of butter. Bake in the oven for 20 minutes. Serve with lemon slices.

SOLE WITH POTATOES AND WINE SAUCE

(SOLE BONNE FEMME – FRANCE)

Cooking time: 35 minutes
Oven temperature: 375°F., 190°C.,
Gas Mark 5

Serves 4

IMPERIAL · METRIC	AMERICAN
4 large or 8 small fillets sole	4 large or 8 small fillets sole
salt	salt
chopped parsley (optional)	chopped parsley (optional)
$\frac{1}{4}$ pint/1$\frac{1}{2}$ dl. white wine	$\frac{2}{3}$ cup white wine
$\frac{1}{4}$ pint/1$\frac{1}{2}$ dl. white sauce (see page 76)	$\frac{2}{3}$ cup white sauce (see page 76)
3–4 oz./75–100 g. mushrooms	about 1 cup mushrooms
1 oz./25 g. butter	2 tablespoons butter

Put the folded fillets of sole in a dish. Add salt and, if wished, a little chopped parsley. Cover with the white wine and buttered papers. Bake in a moderately hot oven for 15 minutes, until just tender. Meanwhile make the white sauce. Slice and fry the mushrooms in the butter, then put into the sauce. Lift the fillets of sole on to a hot dish. Pour the wine liquor from the fish into the sauce, heat and stir briskly until smooth. Thin, if necessary, with more wine and pour over the fish. Garnish with a border of piped mashed potatoes.

BAKED STUFFED RED MULLET
(ROUGET FARCI – FRANCE)

Cooking time: 35–45 minutes
Oven temperature: 375°F., 190°C., Gas Mark 5

Serves 4

IMPERIAL · METRIC	AMERICAN
1 red mullet	1 red mullet or snapper
3 tablespoons soft white breadcrumbs	4 tablespoons soft white bread crumbs
salt and pepper	salt and pepper
3 oz./75 g. butter, melted	6 tablespoons melted butter
2 teaspoons chopped parsley	2 teaspoons chopped parsley
strained juice of 1 small lemon	strained juice of 1 small lemon
parsley	parsley
1 lemon	1 lemon

Wipe the fish, remove scales and slit along the belly. Wash the inside and drain. Mix the breadcrumbs with some salt and pepper, and 2 oz. (50 g., 4 tablespoons) of the butter, parsley and lemon juice to bind. Stuff the fish, press together with the fingers and put into a meat tin. Cover with buttered, greaseproof paper. Bake in the oven until thoroughly cooked. Put the fish on a serving dish and garnish with parsley and lemon slices. Serve with peas.

PILAFF-STUFFED CRAB
(CRABE PILAF – FRANCE)

Cooking time: 15 minutes approximately

Serves 6

IMPERIAL · METRIC	AMERICAN
2 oz./50 g. butter	$\frac{1}{4}$ cup butter
3 oz./75 g. long grain rice, cooked	scant $\frac{1}{2}$ cup long grain rice, cooked
4 tomatoes, skinned and chopped	4 tomatoes, skinned and chopped
2 oz./50 g. sultanas	6 tablespoons seedless white raisins
2 2-lb./1-kg. cooked crabs or 1$\frac{1}{4}$ lb./generous $\frac{1}{2}$ kg. crab meat	2 2-lb. cooked crabs or 1$\frac{1}{4}$ lb. crab meat
salt	salt
freshly ground black pepper	freshly ground black pepper
1 teaspoon chopped parsley	1 teaspoon chopped parsley
strips anchovy fillets to garnish	strips anchovy fillets to garnish
grated Parmesan or Cheddar cheese (optional)	grated Parmesan or Cheddar cheese (optional)

Melt the butter in a pan and add the rice. Stir until the fat is absorbed and then add the tomatoes, sultanas, crab meat, seasoning and parsley. Stir until heated through.

Divide the mixture between the two shells, or if crab meat is used, pile on to a heated dish; garnish with anchovy fillets. If liked, sprinkle with cheese. Serve with a tossed green salad.

GLAZED HERRINGS

(GLASMÄSTARSILL – SWEDEN)

Cooking time: 3–4 minutes

Serves 8–10

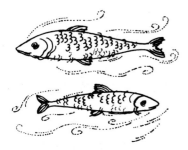

IMPERIAL · METRIC	AMERICAN
2 salted herrings	2 salted herring
1 onion, sliced	1 onion, sliced
$\frac{1}{4}$ leek, sliced	$\frac{1}{4}$ leek, sliced
$\frac{1}{4}$ carrot, sliced	$\frac{1}{4}$ carrot, sliced
2 bay leaves	2 bay leaves
5 white peppercorns	5 white peppercorns
5 allspice	5 allspice
5 cloves	5 cloves
Marinade:	**Marinade:**
$\frac{1}{3}$ pint/2 dl. white wine vinegar	generous $\frac{3}{4}$ cup white wine vinegar
$\frac{1}{2}$ pint/3 dl. water	$1\frac{1}{4}$ cups water
2 oz./50 g. sugar	$\frac{1}{4}$ cup sugar

Clean the fish and soak overnight in cold water. Drain and cut crosswise into $\frac{1}{2}$-inch (1-cm.) slices. Arrange the herrings and other ingredients in alternate layers in a glass jar. Combine the ingredients for the marinade in a saucepan and bring to the boil. Chill and pour over the herring. Leave to stand in a cool place for 1 day. Serve direct from the jar.

BAKED COD AND TOMATOES

(MORUE FLAMANDE – FRANCE)

Cooking time: 50 minutes
Oven temperature: 375°F., 190°C., Gas Mark 5

Serves 8

IMPERIAL · METRIC	AMERICAN
8 portions cod fillet	8 portions cod fillet
2 large onions, sliced	2 large onions, sliced
2 lemons	2 lemons
5 sprigs parsley	5 sprigs parsley
2–3 mushrooms, sliced	2–3 mushrooms, sliced
1 small red pepper, sliced	1 small red sweet pepper, sliced
8 oz./$\frac{1}{4}$ kg. tomatoes, skinned and sliced	$\frac{1}{2}$ lb. tomatoes, skinned and sliced
salt and pepper	salt and pepper
$\frac{1}{2}$ pint/3 dl. dry white wine or cider	$1\frac{1}{4}$ cups dry white wine or cider
1 tablespoon cooked peas	1 tablespoon cooked peas

Wash, skin and dry the fish. Put the onions into a pan, cover with cold water and bring to the boil. Drain the onions and mix with the finely grated lemon rind. Discard all the pith from the lemons and chop the flesh very finely; add to the onions. Chop the parsley, complete with stalks. Mix with the onions, reserving a little for garnish. Add the mushrooms, red pepper and tomatoes.

Butter an ovenproof dish, spread with half the onion mixture, then the fish pieces and top with the rest of the onion mixture. Season very well. Pour in the wine or cider. Cover with buttered paper and bake in the centre of the oven for 45 minutes. Scatter with the green peas and the remaining parsley before serving.

Cassoulet (page 33)

Meat and poultry dishes

Today meat is usually expensive and even difficult to come by in some European countries. So Continental housewives have long since learnt to make the best of the cheaper cuts of meat, and splendidly delicious stews and casseroles are the result. We're all accustomed to Irish stew and Lancashire hot pot, and very good they are, too, but why not try a Goulásh, a Carbonade de Carne or a Cassoulet instead? Just as easy to make, but oh so different.

Indeed, the French can teach us many wonderful ways with meat and poultry. A nation with a world-wide reputation for very high cooking standards, they have produced some classic meat dishes. The Southern European countries have also specialised in the cooking of poultry dishes; we look to them also for delicious veal recipes.

MEAT BALLS
(KÖTTBULLAR – SWEDEN)

Cooking time: 15 minutes

Serves 4–6

IMPERIAL · METRIC	AMERICAN
1 lb./½ kg. minced steak	1 lb. ground steak
4 oz./100 g. pork	¼ lb. pork
8 tablespoons soft white breadcrumbs	generous ½ cup soft white bread crumbs
about 1 pint/6 dl. milk	about 2½ cups milk
salt and pepper	salt and pepper
1 small onion	1 small onion
2 oz./50 g. lard for frying	¼ cup lard or oil for frying
¾ oz./20 g. flour	3 tablespoons all-purpose flour
extra milk	extra milk

Mince the steak and pork twice, so that they are really fine. Soak the breadcrumbs in the milk until it is all absorbed by the crumbs. Squeeze the bread and pour off surplus milk. Season the meat well and mix with the chopped onion, then blend with the soaked breadcrumbs. Shape into small rounds, about ¾ inch (1·5 cm.). Use wet hands and board to help keep the mixture from sticking. Fry in hot lard until brown all over. Turn into a dish and keep hot. Add the flour to the hot fat in the pan, mix well and then stir in sufficient milk to give a thin but coating sauce. Cook until really hot. Pour over the meat balls.

LIVER SKEWERS
(LEBERSPIESSCHEN – SWITZERLAND)

Cooking time: 15 minutes

Serves 4–6

IMPERIAL · METRIC	AMERICAN
1½ lb./¾ kg. calves' liver	1½ lb. calf liver
salt and pepper	salt and pepper
nutmeg	nutmeg
about 12 sage leaves	about 12 sage leaves
about 12 bacon rashers	about 12 bacon slices
4 oz./100 g. butter	½ cup butter

Slice the liver into pieces about 1½ inches (3.5 cm.) long and ½ inch (1 cm.) thick. Season with salt, pepper and nutmeg. Put half a sage leaf on each piece of liver and wrap every piece in a thin, half rasher of bacon. Thread five or six pieces of liver on each skewer and fry in the butter for 15 minutes until cooked through. Serve with boiled potatoes and green beans.

BEEF STROGANOFF
(RUSSIA)

Cooking time: 15–20 minutes

Serves 4

IMPERIAL · METRIC	AMERICAN
1 lb./½ kg. fillet steak	1 lb. beef fillet
2 oz./50 g. butter	¼ cup butter
2 medium onions, sliced	2 medium onions, sliced
4 oz./100 g. mushrooms, sliced	1 cup sliced mushrooms
salt and pepper	salt and pepper
¼ pint/1½ dl. single cream	⅔ cup coffee cream
juice of ½ lemon	juice of ½ lemon

Cut the beef into strips 1½–2 inches (3·5–5 cm.) long and ¼ inch (0·5 cm.) wide. Melt 1 oz. (25 g., 2 tablespoons) of the butter in a frying pan and fry the onions slowly until tender. Add the mushrooms and fry them for a few minutes. Remove the vegetables from the pan, put in the remaining butter and heat gently. Put in the beef strips and fry briskly for 3–4 minutes. Put the onions and mushrooms back into the pan, then season with salt and pepper. Pour in the cream and lemon juice and heat through, for a further minute. Serve with noodles or boiled rice.

CASSEROLE OF BEEF IN BEER
(CARBONADE FLAMANDE – BELGIUM)

Cooking time: 3¾ hours
Oven temperature: 325°F., 170°C., Gas Mark 3

Serves 2–3

IMPERIAL · METRIC	AMERICAN
4 oz./100 g. fat	½ cup shortening or oil
8 oz./¼ kg. onions	½ lb. onions
1 lb./½ kg. stewing steak	1 lb. beef stew meat
2 oz./50 g. flour	½ cup all-purpose flour
½ pint/3 dl. hot beef stock	1¼ cups hot beef stock
½ pint/3 dl. beer	1¼ cups beer
salt and pepper	salt and pepper
1 teaspoon mustard	1 teaspoon mustard

Melt the fat in a frying pan and add the sliced onions; fry them until they begin to turn brown. Cut the stewing steak into eight or ten equal sized pieces. Put the fried onions and steak in alternate layers in a casserole.

Stir the flour into the fat in the frying pan, add the hot stock and beer, and stir well together. Season with salt, pepper and mustard. Gradually bring to the boil, stirring all the time; pour into the casserole over the steak and onions. Cover the casserole before placing in a moderate oven on a low shelf; cook for about 3½ hours.

CHOPPED VEAL
(GESCHNITZELTES KALBFLEISCH – SWITZERLAND)

Cooking time: 10 minutes

Serves 4

IMPERIAL · METRIC	AMERICAN
1 teaspoon chopped onion	1 teaspoon chopped onion
4 oz./100 g. butter	½ cup butter
1 lb./½ kg. lean veal	1 lb. lean veal
salt and pepper	salt and pepper
1 teaspoon lemon juice	1 teaspoon lemon juice

Fry the onion in half the butter until tender, but not brown. Chop all the veal into tiny cubes about ¼ inch (0·5 cm.) thick. Fry in the butter until the meat is cooked. Add the rest of the butter, season well and add lemon juice. Serve with Rösti (see page 58).

BEEF STEW
(GOULÁSH – HUNGARY)

Cooking time: 2 hours

Serves 6

IMPERIAL · METRIC	AMERICAN
1½ lb./¾ kg. beef	1½ lb. beef
2 oz./50 g. dripping	¼ cup drippings
2 onions	2 onions
1½ oz./40 g. flour	6 tablespoons all-purpose flour
1 pint/6 dl. stock	2½ cups stock
¼ pint/1½ dl. beer (optional)	⅔ cup beer (optional)
2 tomatoes	2 tomatoes
pinch salt	pinch salt
1 teaspoon tomato purée	1 teaspoon tomato paste
1 teaspoon paprika pepper	1 teaspoon paprika pepper
bouquet garni (see page 6)	bouquet garni (see page 6)
6 potatoes, peeled and diced	6 potatoes, peeled and diced
2 tablespoons soured cream	3 tablespoons sour cream

Cut the meat into neat pieces and brown in the dripping. Slice the onions and add to the meat. Cook gently until both meat and onions are lightly golden. Sprinkle in the flour and brown. Mix in the stock and beer. Skin and chop the tomatoes, add with the salt, tomato purée, pepper and bouquet garni. Stir well and bring slowly to the boil. Simmer very gently for 1½ hours. Peel and dice the potatoes and add to the goulash after 1 hour. Add the soured cream just before serving.

CASSEROLED OXTAIL
(QUEUE DE BOEUF PAYSANNE – FRANCE)
Illustrated in colour on page 28

Cooking time: 3 hours 15 minutes
Oven temperature: 375°F., 190°C.,
Gas Mark 5

Serves 4

IMPERIAL · METRIC	AMERICAN
4 rashers streaky bacon	4 bacon slices
8 oz./¼ kg. carrots	½ lb. carrots
8 oz./¼ kg. button onions	½ lb. tiny onions
8 oz./¼ kg. young turnips	½ lb. young turnips
2½ oz./65 g. butter	5 tablespoons butter
2½ lb./1¼ kg. oxtail, in pieces	2½ lb. oxtail, in pieces
1 oz./25 g. flour	¼ cup all-purpose flour
¼ pint/1½ dl. red wine	⅔ cup red wine
1½ pints/1 litre stock	3¾ cups stock
salt and pepper	salt and pepper
8 oz./¼ kg. leeks (optional)	½ lb. leeks (optional)
2 sticks celery, sliced	2 stalks celery, sliced
8 oz./¼ kg. mushrooms	½ lb. mushrooms
1 tablespoon chopped parsley	1 tablespoon chopped parsley

Cut the bacon into strips. Scrape and dice two of the carrots. Skin two of the onions and peel and dice one of the turnips. Heat 1½ oz. (40 g.) of the butter in a heavy pan and fry the prepared vegetables and bacon until golden; remove and keep hot.

Brown the oxtail on all sides in the remaining butter. Sprinkle in the flour and cook until brown. Pour in the wine and stock. Season well and turn into a casserole dish with the browned vegetables. Prepare the remaining carrots, onions, turnips, leeks and celery, and trim into neat pieces. Place in the casserole. Cover and cook in the oven for 3 hours. Towards the end of the cooking time, add the prepared mushrooms. Sprinkle with the parsley and serve piping hot.

Casseroled oxtail (page 27)

ROAST VEAL IN CREAM SAUCE

(FYLT KALVESTEK – NORWAY)

Cooking time: 1 hour 50 minutes
Oven temperature: 375°F., 190°C., Gas Mark 5

Serves 6

IMPERIAL · METRIC	AMERICAN
4½ lb./2 kg. loin of veal	4½ lb. veal loin
2 oz./50 g. pork fat	¼ cup fat back
3 oz./75 g. butter	6 tablespoons butter
2 teaspoons salt	2 teaspoons salt
½ pint/3 dl. cream	1¼ cups cream
2 pints/generous 1 litre stock	5 cups stock

Remove any gristle from the veal. Thread thinly cut strips of pork fat through the veal with a larding needle. Brown 2 oz. (50 g., 4 tablespoons) of the butter in a roasting tin. Add the meat and roast for 1 hour in the centre of a moderately hot oven. Turn the meat over and sprinkle with salt. Pour over the cream and stock and roast for a further 45 minutes.
  Strain off the liquid into a pan 10 minutes before cooking time is completed. Bring to the boil, stir in the remainder of the butter over a low heat. Serve as a sauce with the meat.

CHICKEN CASSEROLE

(POLLO IN CASSERUOLA – ITALY)

Cooking time: 1 hour 10 minutes

Serves 4

IMPERIAL · METRIC	AMERICAN
2 young chickens	2 young chickens
salt and pepper	salt and pepper
¼ pint/1½ dl. oil	⅔ cup oil
1 clove garlic	1 clove garlic
8 oz./225 g. lean smoked gammon, diced	1 cup diced lean smoked ham
1 medium onion, finely chopped	1 medium onion, finely chopped
1 small can red peppers (pimento), finely chopped	1 small can red sweet peppers (pimiento), finely chopped

Clean the chickens and joint them into convenient portions. Season with salt and pepper. Heat the oil and crushed clove of garlic in a heavy pan. Remove the garlic when it is brown and add the chicken, turning frequently. When the chicken begins to colour, add the gammon, onion and the peppers. Cover the dish and simmer for 1 hour.

ROSEMARY ROAST LAMB

(GIGOT D'AGNEAU – FRANCE)

Cooking time· approximately 1½–2 hours
Oven temperature: 350°F., 180°C., Gas Mark 4

Serves 8–10

IMPERIAL · METRIC	AMERICAN
1 leg of lamb	1 lamb leg
2–3 cloves garlic	2–3 cloves garlic
few sprigs fresh rosemary	few sprigs fresh rosemary
fat or oil	oil
1 large can flageolets	1 large can flageolets or fava beans

Score the fatty skin of the lamb in a diamond pattern. Cut the garlic in thin slivers; make a small incision at the point of each diamond and insert in this a piece of garlic and a little fresh rosemary.
  Roast the prepared leg with a little fat or oil in a moderate oven allowing 30 minutes per 1 lb. (½ kg.). Place on a warm serving dish and remove the garlic before carving.
  Heat the flageolets according to the instructions on the can and serve with the lamb.

SAUERKRAUT STEW

(BIGOS Z PIECZENI – POLAND)

Cooking time: 1½ hours

Serves 4–6

IMPERIAL · METRIC	AMERICAN
3–4 dried mushrooms	3–4 dried mushrooms
2 lb./1 kg. sauerkraut	2 lb. sauerkraut
4 oz./100 g. salt pork or bacon, diced	½ cup diced fresh picnic shoulder or cured ham or bacon
1 onion, minced	1 onion, ground
1 oz./25 g. flour	¼ cup all-purpose flour
salt and pepper	salt and pepper
8 oz./225 g. leftover beef, veal, pork, lamb (or a combination), diced	1 cup diced leftover beef, veal, pork, lamb (or a combination)
1 teaspoon Worcestershire sauce	1 teaspoon Worcestershire sauce
2 tablespoons Madeira (optional)	3 tablespoons Madeira (optional)

Cook the mushrooms in ½ pint (3 dl., 1¼ cups) water until tender; cut into strips. Combine the sauerkraut and liquid in which the mushrooms cooked. Fry the diced salt pork or bacon. Add the onion and cook until tender. Add the flour and blend until smooth. Combine with the sauerkraut, season and simmer for about 45 minutes. Dice the meat and add to the sauerkraut with the sauce and Madeira. Simmer, tightly covered, for a further 30 minutes.

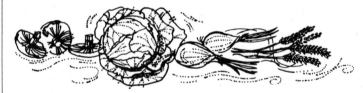

SAUERKRAUT, PORK AND BACON WITH SAUSAGES AND DUMPLINGS

(BAUERNSCHMAUS – AUSTRIA)

Cooking time: 2¾ hours

Serves 6

IMPERIAL · METRIC	AMERICAN
6 loin pork chops	6 loin pork chops
2 lb./1 kg. sauerkraut and juice	2 lb. sauerkraut and juice
beer or water to cover	beer or water to cover
1 teaspoon caraway seeds	1 teaspoon caraway seeds
1–2 cloves garlic	1–2 cloves garlic
salt and pepper	salt and pepper
2 large uncooked potatoes, grated	2 large uncooked potatoes, grated
2 large Spanish onions, sliced	2 large Spanish onions, sliced
2 oz./50 g. lard	¼ cup lard
1 piece back bacon, cubed	1 piece cured ham, cubed
12 frankfurters	12 frankfurters

Simmer the chops with the sauerkraut, beer, caraway seeds, garlic and seasoning, for 1½ hours. Stir in the grated raw potatoes. Cook for 2–3 minutes. Fry the sliced onions in the lard until tender. Add to the sauerkraut with the back bacon and frankfurters. Simmer for 1 hour, adding more water or beer if necessary. Drain the sauerkraut, reserving liquid, and pile on a large wooden platter. Surround with the meat. Serve with large dumplings and hand the gravy separately, seasoned to taste.

SAVOURY LAMB STEAKS
(BÁRÁNY PORKOLT – HUNGARY)

Cooking time: 40 minutes

Serves 4

IMPERIAL · METRIC
4 leg of lamb steaks (1 inch/2·5 cm. thick)
½ pint/3 dl. milk
1 tablespoon vinegar
1 onion, finely chopped
2 bacon rashers, diced
salt and pepper

AMERICAN
4 leg of lamb steaks (1 inch thick)
1¼ cups milk
1 tablespoon vinegar
1 onion, finely chopped
2 bacon slices, diced
salt and pepper

Trim excess fat from the lamb steaks. Leave to soak in the milk and vinegar for about 1 hour, then remove and dry them well. Keep the milk and vinegar. Fry the onion, bacon and lamb until the meat is browned on both sides. Sprinkle with salt and pepper; add the milk and vinegar.

Simmer, covered, for 30 minutes or until the meat is tender. To serve, pour the gravy over the steaks.

PAPRIKA CHICKEN
(PAPRIKAS CSIRKE – HUNGARY)

Cooking time: 30 minutes

Serves 6

IMPERIAL · METRIC
1 chicken (1½–2 lb./¾–1 kg.)
salt to taste
3 oz./75 g. lard
2 medium onions
2 teaspoons paprika pepper
1 teaspoon plain flour
1 carton soured cream

AMERICAN
1 chicken (1½–2 lb.)
salt to taste
6 tablespoons lard
2 medium onions
2 teaspoons paprika pepper
1 teaspoon all-purpose flour
1 carton sour cream

Divide the chicken into neat joints and salt pieces sparingly. Heat the lard and fry the finely chopped onions until golden brown. Mix the paprika with the onion. Put in the chicken pieces and cook gently until tender. Mix the flour with the soured cream and pour over the cooked chicken. Boil for a few minutes, stirring very gently. Serve with small dumplings or macaroni, rice or creamed potatoes, and green salad with French dressing.

VEAL KIDNEYS IN WINE
(ROGNONS DE VEAU SAUTÉ – BELGIUM)

Cooking time: 30 minutes

Serves 2

IMPERIAL · METRIC
4 veal kidneys
1 oz./25 g. butter
4 juniper berries, chopped
salt and pepper to taste
1 tablespoon Burgundy

AMERICAN
4 veal kidneys
2 tablespoons butter
4 juniper berries, chopped
salt and pepper to taste
1 tablespoon Burgundy

Remove most of the fat around the kidneys. Cut the kidneys in thick slices. Heat the butter to sizzling point in a heatproof casserole. Add the kidneys and berries. Brown, covered, over a medium heat, turning kidneys several times. After about 15 minutes, add salt and pepper to taste, and wine. Reheat.

Potato and cheese puffs (page 37)

PORK AND BEAN CASSEROLE

(CASSOULET – FRANCE)
Illustrated in colour on page 24

Cooking time: 3 hours 20 minutes
Oven temperatures: 325°F., 170°C.,
Gas Mark 3; 350°F., 180°C.,
Gas Mark 4

Serves 4–6

IMPERIAL · METRIC	AMERICAN
1 lb./½ kg. lean pork, diced (or ½ lamb and ½ pork)	1 lb. lean pork, diced (or ½ lamb and ½ pork)
4 oz./100 g. bacon trimmings or 1 small garlic sausage, cut in slices	½ cup diced bacon or 1 small garlic sausage, cut in slices
2 medium onions	2 medium onions
8 oz./225 g. tomatoes	½ lb. tomatoes
1 clove garlic	1 clove garlic
1 oz./25 g. lard	2 tablespoons lard
salt and pepper	salt and pepper
4 cloves	4 cloves
6 oz./175 g. soft white breadcrumbs	3 cups soft white bread crumbs
1 (1-lb./450-g.) can haricot beans	1 (1-lb.) can navy beans
chopped parsley	chopped parsley

Cut the pork into 1-inch (2·5-cm.) pieces and dice the bacon trimmings. Peel and quarter the onions and tomatoes. Crush or finely chop the garlic. Melt the lard in a thick-bottomed frying pan. Lightly fry the meat pieces until golden brown, then transfer to an ovenproof casserole.
  Lightly fry the bacon (or sausage slices) and onions and add to the meat. Season with salt and pepper and add the garlic and cloves. Cover with water and sprinkle half the breadcrumbs over the top.
  Cook in the centre of a moderate oven (325°F., 170°C., Gas Mark 3) for 2–3 hours or until the meat is tender. Remove the cloves and stir in the drained beans and tomatoes. Adjust the seasoning and sprinkle the remaining breadcrumbs on top. Return uncovered to the oven (350°F., 180°C., Gas Mark 4) for a further 20 minutes until the breadcrumbs are a golden brown crust. Sprinkle with chopped parsley.

DANISH GINGERED GAMMON

(ROGET SKINKE MED INGEFAER – DENMARK)

Cooking time: 1 hour 55 minutes
Oven temperature: 400°F., 200°C.,
Gas Mark 6

Serves 8

IMPERIAL · METRIC	AMERICAN
4-lb./2-kg. joint gammon	4-lb. piece cured or smoked ham
1 onion, sliced	1 onion, sliced
1 carrot	1 carrot
1 bay leaf	1 bay leaf
6 peppercorns	6 peppercorns
4 oz./100 g. preserved ginger and its syrup	¼ lb. preserved ginger and its syrup
1 teaspoon orange juice	1 teaspoon orange juice

Leave the gammon in water for about 4 hours. Drain. Put into a pan of fresh water with the onion, carrot, bay leaf and peppercorns. Bring to the boil and simmer for 1 hour 40 minutes.
  Drain the joint and take off the rind. Put into a grill pan or roasting tin. Slice the ginger and place the pieces on the top of the joint. Mix the ginger syrup and orange juice and pour over the top. Place the joint in the centre of a moderately hot oven for 15 minutes, basting frequently. Serve with buttered new potatoes and Brussels sprouts or broccoli spears.

POT ROAST

(CARBONADE DE CARNE
ARAGONESA – SPAIN)

Cooking time: 3½ hours

Serves 8–10

IMPERIAL · METRIC	AMERICAN
4-lb./2-kg. joint silverside	4-lb. piece beef round
salt	salt
1 oz./25 g. flour	¼ cup all-purpose flour
3 tablespoons olive oil	scant ¼ cup olive oil
4 onions	4 onions
1 tablespoon chopped parsley	1 tablespoon chopped parsley
1 tablespoon vinegar	1 tablespoon vinegar
1 tablespoon tomato ketchup	1 tablespoon tomato catsup
1 pint/6 dl. water	2½ cups water
½ oz./15 g. plain chocolate	½ square cooking chocolate

Dust the beef with salted flour. Sear all sides in the hot olive oil. Place the meat in a flameproof pot with the sliced onions, parsley, vinegar and ketchup; add the water. Simmer tightly covered for about 3 hours, then remove the meat. Add the chocolate to the sauce, simmer until smooth and serve with the beef.

LAMB STEW

(ARNI KAPAMA – GREECE)

Cooking time: 2 hours

Serves 4

IMPERIAL · METRIC	AMERICAN
1½ oz./40 g. butter	3 tablespoons butter
2 lb./1 kg. leg of lamb, boned	2 lb. boneless lamb leg
2 carrots, sliced	2 carrots, sliced
salt and pepper	salt and pepper
water or stock to cover	water or stock to cover
1 green pepper	1 green sweet pepper
3 tomatoes, skinned and chopped	3 tomatoes, skinned and chopped
2 cartons natural yogurt	2 cartons unflavored yogurt
4 oz./100 g. seedless raisins	¾ cup seedless raisins
little chopped mint	little chopped mint

Melt the butter in a saucepan. Cut the meat into 1-inch (2·5-cm.) pieces. Turn into the saucepan with the carrots. Season well and cover with water or stock. Bring to the boil, cover and simmer for 1 hour. Deseed the pepper, wash and cut into ½-inch (1-cm.) squares. Add the pepper and tomatoes and simmer for a further 1 hour. Add a little more stock if necessary. Before serving, stir the yogurt and raisins into the casserole. Sprinkle with mint and serve at once.

Egg and cheese dishes

Cheese

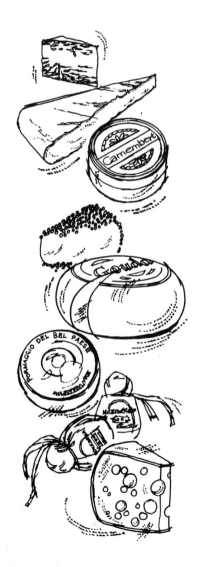

Here are two dairy products with immense culinary possibilities – just think of the French quiche Lorraine, a truly wonderful cheese tart; or the omelette with its countless variations.

When times were hard and meat scarce, eggs and cheese came into their own – as a result there are innumerable gourmet Continental dishes made from them without breaking the household bank!

While no one would dispute the quality and flavour of our own English cheeses, this does not mean that we should turn our heads away from the many delicious Continental cheeses available. Here are a few of them:

Denmark
Samsoe A golden wheel-shaped cheese.
Danish Blue or Danablu Milder than Gorgonzola.

France
Brie Soft-textured and sold cut in wedges. Perishable.
Camembert Well known soft cheese of Normandy. When it yields to pressure with the fingers it is ready to eat.
Demi-sel A cream cheese that is best eaten fresh for full enjoyment.
Tomme au raisin The rind is covered with black grape skins and seeds from the local wine pressings. White and mild in flavour.
Port Salut A mild and slightly salty cheese, originally made by monks; indeed, it still is in northwest France.
Roquefort Blue veined cheese. Matured from sheeps' milk in the caves in Roquefort, where cheese making has been practised for 2,000 years.

Holland
Edam Ball-shaped and covered in red wax. Mild and can be used for cooking.
Gouda A golden, wheel-shaped cheese. The young cheese is very mild and as it matures it gets stronger. More flavour than Edam.

Italy
Bel Paese A soft creamy cheese.
Gorgonzola Sharp, spicy blue cheese.
Mozzarella The correct cheese to use for making pizza. It has a sweet-sour flavour.
Parmesan Very hard cheese, good for grating and keeps well.

Switzerland
Emmenthal Delicious cheese with walnut-sized holes in it.
Gruyère The holes in Gruyère cheese are about the size of hazelnuts. Excellent for cooking.
Swiss processed This must be mentioned here because as well as being good at making cheese, the Swiss also excel in the art of processing cheese.

Eggs

It was an old boast of the French that they had found 685 ways of cooking eggs! Probably they evolved many of these recipes during the days of fast in the French Courts. Here are a few French recipes:

EN COCOTTE

Cocotte dishes are shallow earthenware dishes with two small ears or a handle. Alternatively, use ramekins which are tiny soufflé dishes.
Warm the buttered dishes and break in the eggs. Put the dishes into a pan or tin half-filled with warm water, and cover the dishes with a lid or foil. Bake in the centre of a moderate oven (350°F., 180°C., Gas Mark 4) for about 8 minutes until the whites are set and the yolks creamy. The eggs will go on cooking for a while after you take them out of the oven, so take them out just before they are set. Season and serve.

Oeufs en cocotte à la crème
Put a tablespoon of cream into the cocotte before adding the egg. Dot with a little butter and season well before serving.

Oeufs en cocotte au Parmesan
As basic method, but sprinkle with a little grated Parmesan cheese before baking.

Oeufs en cocotte Mornay
Put a spoonful of cheese sauce in the cocotte, then add the egg and top with more cheese sauce and a little grated cheese. Bake.

OEUFS SUR LE PLAT

Eggs 'sur le plat' are eggs baked in round shallow earthenware or metal dishes with two handles or ears. Preferably use dishes for individual eggs.
Warm and butter the dishes. Break eggs in and bake in the centre of a moderate oven (350°F., 180°C., Gas Mark 4) for 5–7 minutes until eggs are only just setting – they should be taken out of the oven just before they are cooked.

Oeufs Florentine
Prepare a bed of cooked spinach. Put a little cheese sauce over the spinach. Break the eggs into hollows made in the spinach, sprinkle with cheese and grill quickly.

Oeufs à la Lorraine
Line the dish with lightly fried or grilled bacon rashers and very thinly sliced Gruyère cheese. Add the eggs, pour over some cream and bake.

Oeufs Bercy
Prepare the eggs as in the basic method, then garnish with small fried sausages and pour round tomato sauce.

BAKED CHEESE
(RAMEQUIN MIT KÄSESCHEIBEN – SWITZERLAND)

Cooking time: 30 minutes
Oven temperature: 350°F., 180°C., Gas Mark 4

Serves 4–6

IMPERIAL · METRIC	AMERICAN
12 slices bread	12 slices bread
12 slices Emmenthal cheese	12 slices Emmenthal cheese
2 eggs	2 eggs
1 pint/6 dl. milk	2½ cups milk
½ teaspoon grated nutmeg	½ teaspoon grated nutmeg

Arrange the bread and cheese in overlapping layers in a buttered pie dish. Blend the eggs and milk together with the nutmeg and pour into the dish. Stand the dish in a pan of water. Bake in the centre of a moderate oven for about 30 minutes or until the milk is absorbed. Serve immediately.

QUICHE LORRAINE
(FRANCE)

Cooking time: 40 minutes
Oven temperature: 375°F., 190°C.,
Gas Mark 5

Serves 6

IMPERIAL · METRIC	AMERICAN
4 oz./100 g. shortcrust pastry	basic pie dough using 1 cup all-purpose flour, etc.
4 bacon rashers	4 bacon slices
½ small onion, finely chopped	½ small onion, finely chopped
2 oz./50 g. Emmenthal or Cheshire cheese, thinly sliced	2 oz. Emmenthal or Cheshire cheese, thinly sliced
2 small eggs	2 eggs
¼ pint/1½ dl. creamy milk	⅔ cup milk or coffee cream
salt and cayenne pepper	salt and cayenne pepper
½ oz./15 g. butter, melted	1 tablespoon melted butter
2–3 tomatoes, skinned and sliced	2–3 tomatoes, skinned and sliced

Line a 7-inch (18-cm.) flan ring with the pastry, neaten the edges and prick the base with a fork. Cut off bacon rinds and fry the bacon with the onion. Snip the bacon into pieces and arrange in the pastry-lined flan ring. Add the onion and the slices of cheese. Beat the eggs lightly with the milk; season well with salt and cayenne pepper. Add the melted butter and strain the mixture into the flan case. Arrange slices of tomato in a circle.

Bake on the centre shelf of the oven for 40 minutes. Cut into slices and serve hot or cold.

POTATO AND CHEESE PUFFS
(GOUDA BOLLETJES – HOLLAND)
Illustrated in colour on page 32

Cooking time: 35 minutes

Makes about 30

IMPERIAL · METRIC	AMERICAN
1 lb./½ kg. potatoes	1 lb. potatoes
salt and pepper	salt and pepper
½ oz./15 g. unsalted butter	1 tablespoon sweet butter
4 tablespoons water	⅓ cup water
1½ oz./40 g. plain flour	generous ¼ cup all-purpose flour
1 egg	1 egg
3 oz./75 g. Gouda cheese, grated	¾ cup grated Gouda cheese
fat for deep frying	oil for deep frying

Peel the potatoes and cook in a pan of boiling salted water until tender. Drain well, sieve and season well. Make a choux paste by bringing the butter and water to the boil. Add the flour all at once and beat over a gentle heat until the mixture forms a ball. Cool slightly. Beat the egg into the paste gradually and continue beating well until the paste becomes elastic and no longer sticks to the sides of the pan. Add the potatoes and half the cheese.

Put teaspoonfuls of the mixture into the hot fat. Cook the puffs until they are golden brown and crisp. Pile on to a heated dish, sprinkle with the remaining cheese and serve at once.

CHEESE FONDUE
(SWITZERLAND)

Cooking time: 30 minutes

Serves 1

IMPERIAL · METRIC	AMERICAN
1 clove garlic	1 clove garlic
6 oz./175 g. Emmenthal or Gruyère cheese (or both)	1½ cups grated Emmenthal or Gruyère cheese (or both)
6 tablespoons white wine	½ cup white wine
½ oz./15 g. butter	1 tablespoon butter
4 tablespoons Kirsch	⅓ cup Kirsch
1 teaspoon cornflour	1 teaspoon cornstarch
pepper	pepper
pinch grated nutmeg	pinch grated nutmeg
pinch bicarbonate of soda	pinch baking soda

Rub the clove of garlic round the inside of the fondue dish. Crush the clove and leave in the dish. Grate in the cheese and add the wine and butter. Heat very slowly using a wooden spoon. Bring to bubbling point, blend the Kirsch with the cornflour and stir into the cheese. Add pepper, grated nutmeg and bicarbonate of soda. Put the fondue on the table over a spirit lamp. Regulate to allow the fondue to 'shiver' slightly but not boil. Serve the fondue with a basket of large, bite size cubes of bread with crusts on.

The guests spike these on forks, dip them in the fondue and stir two or three times. If the bread is dropped in the fondue by a guest, he must buy the company a bottle of wine!

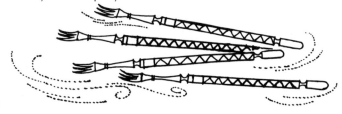

CHEESE SAVOURY
(GNOCCHI – ITALY)

Cooking time: 40 minutes
Oven temperature: 375°F., 190°C., Gas Mark 5

Serves 4

IMPERIAL · METRIC	AMERICAN
1 pint/6 dl. milk	2½ cups milk
1 onion, skinned	1 onion, skinned
1 bay leaf	1 bay leaf
4 oz./100 g. semolina	scant ¾ cup semolina flour or farina
salt and pepper	salt and pepper
2 oz./50 g. Parmesan or Cheddar cheese, grated	½ cup grated Parmesan or Cheddar cheese
½ oz./15 g. butter	1 tablespoon butter
1 teaspoon French mustard	1 teaspoon French mustard

Put the milk into a pan; add the onion and bay leaf and bring slowly to the boil. Take from the heat and remove the onion and bay leaf. Sprinkle in the semolina and seasoning; simmer until thick, stirring well. Remove from the heat, stir in 1½ oz. (40 g., ⅓ cup) of the cheese; add the butter and mustard. Spread evenly about ¾ inch (1·5 cm.) thick on a cold surface.

When cooled, cut into small squares. Arrange in a buttered dish, dust with extra cheese, and brown in a moderately hot oven for 30 minutes on the top shelf.

POACHED EGGS ON YOGURT

(PARZHENI YAITZA NA OCHI
VARAV KISSELO MLYAKO –
BULGARIA)

Cooking time: 10 minutes

Serves 4

IMPERIAL · METRIC
1 pint/6 dl. natural yogurt
2 cloves garlic
salt
½ tablespoon vinegar
4 eggs
1½ oz./40 g. butter
paprika pepper

AMERICAN
2½ cups unflavored yogurt
2 cloves garlic
salt
½ tablespoon vinegar
4 eggs
3 tablespoons butter
paprika pepper

Beat the yogurt well, crush the garlic and add with the salt and vinegar.
Pour the mixture into four individual bowls. Poach the eggs in the usual
way and put one in each bowl carefully. Melt the butter, pour over the
eggs, sprinkle with salt and paprika pepper.

POACHED EGGS ON SPINACH

(UOVA ALLA FIORENTINA – ITALY)

Cooking time: 15 minutes

Serves 4

IMPERIAL · METRIC
1 oz./25 g. butter
2 lb./1 kg. cooked chopped
    spinach, well drained
grated nutmeg
8 eggs
½ pint/3 dl. cheese sauce (see
    page 76)
grated cheese

AMERICAN
2 tablespoons butter
2 lb. cooked chopped spinach,
    well drained
grated nutmeg
8 eggs
1¼ cups cheese sauce (see page
    76)
grated cheese

Add the butter to the cooked spinach and divide between four
individual, buttered ovenproof dishes. Sprinkle with grated nutmeg.
Poach the eggs, drain well and place on the spinach. Cover the eggs
with cheese sauce, sprinkle grated cheese on top and brown quickly
under a very hot grill. Serve at once.

EGGS STUFFED WITH PRAWNS

(OEUFS FARCIS AUX CREVETTES –
FRANCE)

Cooking time: 20 minutes

Serves 4

IMPERIAL · METRIC
4 eggs
4 anchovies
12 large prawns
2 oz./50 g. butter
salt and cayenne pepper
hot tomato sauce to serve (see
    page 52 or 77)

AMERICAN
4 eggs
4 anchovies
12 large prawns or shrimp
¼ cup butter
salt and cayenne pepper
hot tomato sauce to serve (see
    page 52 or 77)

Hard-boil and shell the eggs and cut in half lengthways, scoop out the
yolks into a basin. Add the anchovies and half the shelled prawns. Mash
together, then pass through a sieve. Add the butter, salt, cayenne
pepper and mix thoroughly. Place a spoonful into the hard-boiled whites
of eggs. Place a prawn head in the centre of each. Put into a buttered
ovenproof dish and spoon the rest of the filling into the centre of the
dish. Grill for about 5 minutes. Spoon hot tomato sauce around the eggs.

TINY SOUFFLÉS

(SALZBURGER NOCKERLN –
AUSTRIA)

Cooking time: 5 minutes
Oven temperature: 475°F., 240°C.,
Gas Mark 9

Serves 2

IMPERIAL · METRIC	AMERICAN
3 egg yolks and 4 egg whites	3 egg yolks and 4 egg whites
1 teaspoon icing sugar	1 teaspoon confectioners' sugar
1 teaspoon flour	1 teaspoon all-purpose flour
½ oz./15 g. butter	1 tablespoon butter

Turn the oven on. Put an ovenproof omelette pan over a small flame. Separate the egg yolks and whites. Whisk the egg yolks very lightly with a fork until well blended. Whisk the egg whites until very stiff, add the icing sugar and whisk until smooth. Fork the egg yolks into the egg whites and fold in the flour.

Put the butter into the hot omelette pan and turn up the heat. Wait until the butter foams, then drop in half the egg mixture in three large 'blobs'. Make the 'blobs' high rather than wide and keep them apart. Leave over medium heat for about ½ minute until the underneath parts of the nockerln have set, then put the omelette pan quickly into the very hot oven. Leave for 2 minutes until the tops of the nockerln have browned lightly. Repeat with the remaining mixture. Remove nockerln carefully with a palette knife and arrange them on a hot dish. Dust liberally with icing sugar and serve at once. The centre should be light and creamy, the outside golden brown and puffed.

EGG AND ONION CASSEROLE

(ÄGG OCH LÖKGRYTA – SWEDEN)

Cooking time: 20 minutes
Oven temperature: 450°F., 230°C.,
Gas Mark 8

Serves 4

IMPERIAL · METRIC	AMERICAN
2 large onions	2 large onions
3 oz./75 g. butter	6 tablespoons butter
6 hard-boiled eggs	6 hard-cooked eggs
3 oz./75 g. flour	¾ cup all-purpose flour
¾ pint/4 dl. milk	scant 2 cups milk
2 oz./50 g. cheese, grated	½ cup grated cheese
salt and pepper	salt and pepper

Skin, slice and fry the onions in 1 oz. (25 g., 2 tablespoons) butter. Turn into a casserole dish. Shell and slice the eggs and spread over the onions. Melt the remaining butter in a saucepan and stir in the flour. Gradually add the milk, stirring all the time. Allow to simmer for 5 minutes.

Stir in two-thirds of the grated cheese and season. Pour the sauce into the casserole. Top with the remaining cheese. Bake in a hot oven for 10 minutes, or under a grill until slightly brown on top.

FRIED BREAD AND CHEESE

(KÄSESCHNITTEN BASLER ART –
SWITZERLAND)

Cooking time: 10 minutes

Serves 4

IMPERIAL · METRIC	AMERICAN
7–8 oz./200–225 g. Emmenthal cheese	about ½ lb. Emmenthal cheese
10–14 oz./275–350 g. stale bread	scant ¾ lb. stale bread
¾ pint/4 dl. milk and water	scant 2 cups milk and water
1 onion	1 onion
1 oz./25 g. butter	2 tablespoons butter
pepper	pepper

Cut the Emmenthal and bread in thin pieces. Heat the milk and water. Place the bread and cheese pieces in a bowl and pour the heated liquid over. Leave to stand. Meanwhile, grate the onion finely and fry in the butter in a frying pan. Add the cheese and bread which should have soaked up all the liquid by now.

Fry on a low heat, turning until golden brown. Dust with a little pepper before serving.

SAVOURY OMELETTE
(FRANCE)

Cooking time: 5 minutes

Serves 2

IMPERIAL · METRIC	AMERICAN
3 large eggs	3 large eggs
salt and pepper	salt and pepper
1 tablespoon water	1 tablespoon water
1 tablespoon milk	1 tablespoon milk
¾ oz./20 g. butter or 1 tablespoon cooking oil	1½ tablespoons butter or 1 tablespoon cooking oil
filling as liked, prepared in advance	filling as liked, prepared in advance
sprigs of parsley and tomato slices	sprigs of parsley and tomato slices

Break the eggs into a bowl. Season and add the water and milk. Beat lightly with a fork.

Heat a 6-inch (15-cm.) omelette pan or frying pan, put the butter or cooking oil into the pan to become really hot – do not let it brown. Pour in the egg mixture. Using a fork, draw the mixture from the sides of the pan into the centre. Allow the omelette mixture to set as quickly as possible. When it is still slightly runny on top, spoon on the filling and fold in half, or fold into three, envelope fashion.

Garnish with parsley sprigs and tomato slices.

DESSERT SOUFFLÉ OMELETTE
(FRANCE)

Cooking time: 6–8 minutes
Oven temperature: 350°F., 180°C., Gas Mark 4

Serves 2

IMPERIAL · METRIC	AMERICAN
4 eggs	4 eggs
2 teaspoons castor sugar	2 teaspoons sugar
1 teaspoon vanilla essence	1 teaspoon vanilla extract
1 oz./25 g. butter	2 tablespoons butter
jam or stewed fruit to fill	jam, jelly or stewed fruit to fill
castor sugar for dredging	sugar for dredging

Separate the eggs. Beat the yolks lightly with the castor sugar and vanilla essence. Lightly fold in the stiffly whisked egg whites.

Melt the butter in a 6-inch (15-cm.) omelette pan. When hot, pour in the egg mixture. Set for 1 minute over a gentle heat. Finish cooking either under a hot grill for 2 minutes or in a moderate oven for 5–6 minutes. Cut quickly across the centre (cut only half-way through) and pour in a filling of jam or stewed fruit. Fold over and turn on to a hot dish. Dredge with sugar and decorate, if possible, with criss-cross lines made with a hot skewer. Serve immediately.

STUFFED EGGS WITH SARDINES

(AEG MED SARDINFYLD – DENMARK)

No cooking

Serves 6

IMPERIAL · METRIC	AMERICAN
6 hard-boiled eggs	6 hard-cooked eggs
1 small can sardines	1 small can sardines
1–2 tablespoons mayonnaise	2 tablespoons mayonnaise
salt and pepper	salt and pepper
tomato, gherkin, stuffed olive or radishes	tomato, sweet dill pickle, stuffed olive or radishes
lettuce leaves	lettuce leaves
rye crispbread	rye crispbread

Shell the eggs and cut in half lengthways. Carefully remove the yolks and sieve them into a basin. Drain the sardines and add to the yolks with sufficient mayonnaise to mix to a creamy consistency. Season. Pipe or spoon the mixture back into the egg whites.

Decorate with small shapes of tomato, gherkin, stuffed olive or radish. Place on lettuce leaves and serve on crispbread.

Variations
The following can be added to the sieved yolks and mayonnaise:
Shrimp 2 oz. (50 g.) very finely chopped shrimps and 1 teaspoon anchovy essence.
Curry 2 teaspoons curry powder.
Tomato 2 teaspoons tomato purée.

SCRAMBLED EGGS WITH VEGETABLES

(HUEVOS REVUELTOS AL PISTO – SPAIN)

Cooking time: 10 minutes

Serves 4

IMPERIAL · METRIC	AMERICAN
2 tablespoons olive oil	3 tablespoons olive oil
1 onion, peeled and chopped	1 onion, peeled and chopped
1 tomato, peeled and chopped	1 tomato, peeled and chopped
½ green pepper, seeded and chopped	½ green sweet pepper, seeded and chopped
2 courgettes, sliced	2 small zucchini, sliced
¼ teaspoon salt	¼ teaspoon salt
6 eggs	6 eggs

Heat the olive oil. Add the onion, tomato, green pepper and courgettes. Sprinkle with salt. When the vegetables are tender, turn off the heat. Beat the eggs and quickly stir them into the vegetables.

STUFFED FRIED PANCAKES

(BLINTZES – RUSSIA)

Cooking time: 10 minutes

Serves 2–4

IMPERIAL · METRIC	AMERICAN
4 oz./100 g. plain flour	1 cup all-purpose flour
1 teaspoon baking powder	1 teaspoon baking powder
pinch salt	pinch salt
2 eggs	2 eggs
¼ pint/about 1½ dl. milk	⅔ cup milk
8 oz./225 g. cottage cheese	1 cup cottage cheese
1 egg, beaten	1 egg, beaten
grated rind of 1 lemon	grated rind of 1 lemon
2 tablespoons castor sugar	3 tablespoons sugar
2 oz./50 g. butter	¼ cup butter

Make a batter by sifting together the flour, baking powder and salt, and adding the eggs and the milk. Beat thoroughly. Heat a thick, buttered frying pan and make pancakes in the usual way. Blend together the sieved cottage cheese, beaten egg, lemon rind and the sugar and spoon an equal amount of the filling into the middle of each pancake. Fold over like an envelope and fry in the butter until golden brown.

Serve with soured cream and soft brown sugar mixed with powdered cinnamon.

TOASTED STUFFED LOAVES
(PAN RELLANADO – SPAIN)

Cooking time: 15 minutes

Serves 4

IMPERIAL · METRIC	AMERICAN
1 long French loaf or 2 Vienna loaves	1 long French loaf
good $\frac{1}{2}$ pint/generous 3 dl. olive oil	generous 1$\frac{1}{4}$ cups olive oil
4 oz./100 g. bacon	6 bacon slices
4 eggs	4 eggs
1 medium can tomatoes	1 medium can tomatoes
salt and pepper	salt and pepper
2 onions, sliced	2 onions, sliced
2 oz./50 g. cheese, grated	$\frac{1}{2}$ cup grated cheese

Slice the loaf or loaves lengthwise and divide into four equal sections. Place under the grill, crusty side up, until toasted. Remove and discard part of the soft inside.

Soak the loaves thoroughly with olive oil and return to the grill, soft side up, and grill to a light golden colour. Add the bacon in small slices, using it to prevent the sides and tops of the hollowed loaves being burnt. Meanwhile, beat the eggs with the canned tomatoes, and add salt and pepper to taste. Pour into the hollows in the loaves, top with a layer of onion rings and grated cheese and cook until the mixture has set.

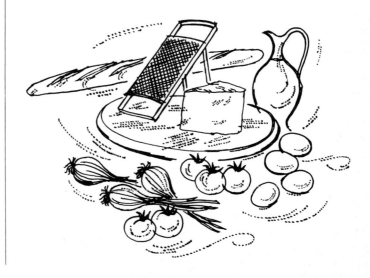

Rice and pasta dishes

Savoury rice dishes and pasta are native to the southern part of Europe, but their popularity is spreading and now we enjoy them as much as the Italians or Spaniards.

The paella of Spain or a really delicious pilaff are hard to beat. So simple to prepare, too, and yet they have just the right exotic touch for a party. In this chapter there are also some lesser known dishes for you to try and savour.

It is as well to know a little more about the various pasta and rices available and the following section will tell you all you need to know. You will find also a section on how to cook pasta and rice to perfection – just like the Southern Europeans!

Pasta

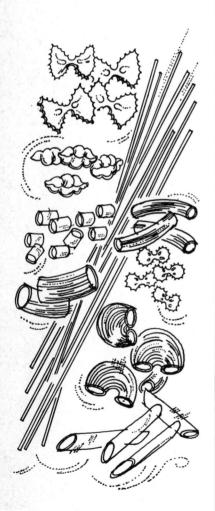

There are a great many types of pasta. To list all the Italian names for the various shapes available would take a great deal of space; also many excellent pasta shapes are now made here in England and sold under English names.

Pasta is a mixture of flour and water and, occasionally, egg too. It is made into an infinite variety of sizes and shapes. Some are more suited to one recipe than to another, but many are interchangeable. Some are eaten with sauce, some are stuffed and some are served in soup.

Here is a short list of a few of the better known pasta varieties available here:

Alfabeto The letters of the alphabet.
Bucatini Very thin macaroni.
Cannelloni Thinly rolled squares of pasta to be stuffed with a savoury filling and rolled up.
Capellini Very thin macaroni.
Conchigue Little shells.
Ditali Cut tubes of large macaroni.
Farfalletti Butterfly shapes in various sizes.
Gnocchi Small semolina dumplings.
Lasagne Ribbon-like spaghetti.
Macaroni Covers the larger pasta varieties, generally tubular, but can also refer to shells, grills, wheels, etc.
Manicotti Rather similar to cannelloni.
Pastina Tiny round shapes.
Ravioli Stuffed squares of pasta.
Rigatoni Ribbed macaroni.
Spaghetti Long, round and with no holes.
Vermicelli Long, thin pasta.

How to cook pasta

Using the largest pan you have, first bring the salted water to the boil, then add all the pasta at once. If it is long, don't break it but curl it round in the pan as it softens in the water, or push it down with a spoon.

Cook for 6–15 minutes depending on the size. In any event, start testing after about 5 minutes by pressing a piece with your thumb nail. If it is tender, but still firm, it is ready.

Drain it and serve at once. Beware of overcooking and never keep pasta hot. One pint (6 dl., 2½ cups) of sauce is enough for 1 lb. (½ kg.) of pasta, and this amount of pasta will serve four people as a main course.

Rice

The Italians are masters of rice cookery. Never do they produce the tasteless plain boiled variety that is sometimes offered at English tables; they cook it to perfection and, like their pasta, they know how to blend and flavour it.

Washing most packeted rice does it little, if any good; pick it over and quickly dip it once or twice in cold water before drying it in a clean cloth.

The easy one-two-one method of cooking rice

Use 1 cup of rice to 2 cups of water or stock, and 1 teaspoon of salt. It doesn't matter what cup you use as long as the same size is used for measuring both rice and liquid.

Put the rice into a buttered pan with the water and salt, bring it to the boil and stir once only. Cover with a well fitting lid and simmer for about 15 minutes, without stirring. Serve, fluffing lightly with a fork, not a spoon.

For four people you will need 8 oz. (225 g., ½ lb.) rice.

To fry rice

In a frying pan, melt 1 oz. (25 g., 2 tablespoons) butter, or use oil or both. Add a chopped onion and rice (1 cup of rice to 2 cups of liquid) and fry gently until lightly golden. Add the boiling liquid, which can be water or stock. Bring to the boil, stir and cook for 15 minutes, covered with a well fitting lid. Fluff with a fork.

EGG NOODLES AND TOMATO SAUCE

(FETTUCINE ALLA MARINARA – ITALY)

Cooking time: 25 minutes

Serves 4

IMPERIAL · METRIC	AMERICAN
2 tablespoons olive oil	3 tablespoons olive oil
2 medium onions, sliced	2 medium onions, sliced
2 cloves garlic, finely chopped	2 cloves garlic, finely chopped
1 lb./½ kg. ripe tomatoes, skinned and chopped, or 1 14-oz./396-g. can peeled tomatoes	1 lb. ripe tomatoes, skinned and chopped, or 1 14-oz. can peeled tomatoes
1 level teaspoon dried basil	1 level teaspoon dried basil
finely ground black pepper	finely ground black pepper
8 oz./225 g. egg noodles	½ lb. egg noodles
6 anchovy fillets, chopped	6 anchovy fillets, chopped

Heat the oil and fry the onions until tender. Add the garlic and cook for 1 minute. Stir in the tomatoes and basil. Season well with pepper. Continue cooking over gentle heat for about 10 minutes.

Meanwhile, put the egg noodles into well salted boiling water. Cook until tender – about 15 minutes; drain well. Add the anchovies to the sauce and cook for another 4–5 minutes.

Pile the noodles into a hot bowl and pour on the sauce or serve it separately. Hand round a bowl of grated cheese.

RIBBON NOODLES AND HAM

(TAGLIATELLE AL PROSCIUTTO – ITALY)

Cooking time: 25 minutes

Serves 4

IMPERIAL · METRIC	AMERICAN
8 oz./225 g. narrow ribbon noodles	½ lb. narrow ribbon noodles
3 oz./75 g. unsalted butter	6 tablespoons sweet butter
6–8 oz./175–225 g. prosciutto (raw smoked ham), chopped	¾–1 cup chopped prosciutto (raw smoked ham)
3 tablespoons grated Parmesan cheese	scant ¼ cup grated Parmesan cheese

Put the noodles on to cook in boiling, salted water until just tender. Melt the butter in a sauté pan, without letting it brown. Add the ham. Drain the noodles and add to the butter and ham. Mix in the Parmesan and serve immediately.

MACARONI IN TOMATO AND CHEESE SAUCE

(MACCHERONI ALLA NAPOLETANA – ITALY)

Cooking time: 25 minutes

Serves 6

IMPERIAL · METRIC	AMERICAN
10 oz./275 g. macaroni	scant ¾ lb. macaroni
2½ oz./60 g. butter	5 tablespoons butter
½ small onion, sliced	½ small onion, sliced
2 lb./1 kg. tomatoes, skinned and sliced	2 lb. tomatoes, skinned and sliced
salt and pepper	salt and pepper
½ teaspoon chopped basil	½ teaspoon chopped basil
1 oz./25 g. grated Parmesan cheese	¼ cup grated Parmesan cheese
extra grated Parmesan cheese for serving	extra grated Parmesan cheese for serving

Cook the macaroni in 5 pints (3 litres, 6½ pints) boiling, salted water. Simmer for 20 minutes; drain, rinse and drain again. Melt half the butter and lightly fry the onion until tender, but not brown. Add the tomatoes, salt, pepper and basil. Cook for 5 minutes, add the rest of the butter, the cheese and the macaroni. Stir over the heat for 5 minutes. Serve with more grated Parmesan cheese.

SPAGHETTI BOLOGNESE

(ITALY)

Cooking time: 25 minutes

Serves 3–4

IMPERIAL · METRIC	AMERICAN
½ oz./15 g. cooking fat	1 tablespoon oil
8 oz./225 g. minced beef	½ lb. ground beef
1 small onion, chopped	1 small onion, chopped
¾ pint/4 dl. water	scant 2 cups water
1 packet tomato soup	1 package tomato soup mix
½ teaspoon salt and pepper	½ teaspoon salt and pepper
1 bay leaf	1 bay leaf
8 oz./225 g. spaghetti	½ lb. spaghetti

Melt the cooking fat in a pan and lightly fry the beef and onion. Add the water and the soup powder, stir until the mixture thickens. Add the seasoning and the bay leaf and simmer gently for 20 minutes. Cook the spaghetti according to the directions on the packet. Remove the bay leaf and pour the sauce over the hot, drained spaghetti.

STUFFED PASTA ROLLS

(CANNELLONI DI MAGRO – ITALY)

Cooking time: 25 minutes
Oven temperature: 325°F., 170°C.,
Gas Mark 3

Serves 4

IMPERIAL · METRIC	AMERICAN
4 oz./100 g. plain flour	1 cup all-purpose flour
2 eggs	2 eggs
pinch salt	pinch salt
4 tablespoons chopped cooked spinach	5 tablespoons chopped cooked spinach
2 tablespoons cream cheese	3 tablespoons cream cheese
1 tablespoon cottage cheese	1 tablespoon cottage cheese
1 egg yolk	1 egg yolk
salt and pepper	salt and pepper
2 oz./50 g. butter, melted	$\frac{1}{4}$ cup butter, melted
2 tablespoons grated Parmesan cheese	3 tablespoons grated Parmesan cheese

Make a well in the sifted flour, add the eggs, salt and mix to a dough. Put on to a floured board and knead very well until smooth. Roll out finely and cut into 4-inch (10-cm.) squares. Boil in a large saucepan of water for 5–8 minutes. Remove carefully and lay on a cloth to dry.

Mix the remaining ingredients well together, except the butter and Parmesan cheese. Put a tablespoon of the stuffing on each square. Roll up the cannelloni and lay them in a fireproof dish, pour on the melted butter and sprinkle Parmesan cheese on top.

Put in a moderate oven for 15 minutes until heated through. Serve at once.

RICE AND CHEESE DISH

(RISOTTO ALLA MILANESE – ITALY)

Cooking time: 25 minutes

Serves 6

IMPERIAL · METRIC	AMERICAN
12 oz./350 g. long grain rice	scant 2 cups long grain rice
1 small onion, finely chopped	1 small onion, finely chopped
4 oz./100 g. butter	$\frac{1}{2}$ cup butter
1 marrow bone	1 marrow bone
3 pints/1$\frac{1}{2}$ litres stock	7$\frac{1}{2}$ cups stock
$\frac{1}{4}$ pint/1$\frac{1}{2}$ dl. dry white wine	$\frac{2}{3}$ cup dry white wine
$\frac{1}{2}$ teaspoon powdered saffron	$\frac{1}{2}$ teaspoon powdered saffron
4 oz./100 g. grated Parmesan cheese	1 cup grated Parmesan cheese
salt and pepper	salt and pepper

Wash and dry the rice thoroughly. Fry the onion in 2 oz. (50 g., $\frac{1}{4}$ cup) of the butter until tender, but not browned. Add the marrow from the bone. Add the rice and cook gently for a few minutes, stirring continuously. Pour in the boiling stock.

Cook for 10 minutes, add the wine and saffron; mix well. Cook slowly for another 5 minutes when all the stock should be absorbed. Remove from the heat. Add the rest of the butter and 3 oz. (75 g., $\frac{3}{4}$ cup) of the cheese.

Season and mix well together. Sprinkle with the rest of the cheese and allow to stand for a few minutes before serving.

PAELLA
(SPAIN)

Cooking time: 35 minutes

Serves 4

IMPERIAL · METRIC	AMERICAN
3 tablespoons olive oil	scant ¼ cup olive oil
½ clove garlic, crushed	½ clove garlic, crushed
1 small onion, finely sliced	1 small onion, finely sliced
¼ small cooked chicken	¼ small cooked chicken
1 canned red pepper (pimento)	1 canned red pepper (pimiento)
1 6-oz./170-g. can tomatoes	1 6-oz. can tomatoes
8 oz./225 g. long grain rice, unwashed	generous 1 cup long grain rice, unwashed
salt and pepper	salt and pepper
about ¾ pint/4 dl. chicken stock	scant 2 cups chicken stock
½ teaspoon saffron	½ teaspoon saffron
½ pint/3 dl. mussels, cooked and shelled	1¼ cups mussels, cooked and shelled
1 small packet frozen peas, cooked	1 small package frozen peas, cooked
1 small can artichoke hearts	1 small can artichoke hearts
½ pint/3 dl. shelled prawns	1¼ cups shelled prawns or shrimp
4 oz./100 g. mushrooms, sliced	1 cup sliced mushrooms
1 small can lobster meat	1 small can lobster meat

Heat the oil in a large saucepan and add the garlic and onion. Cook until tender but not brown. Remove and keep hot. Chop the chicken and brown in the oil. Keep hot, with the onion. Add the pepper and drained tomatoes to the pan with the rice. Stir until the rice just begins to brown. Season well. Add as much stock as the rice will absorb. Add the chicken and the onion.

   Cook slowly for 15 minutes. Stir in the saffron, drained mussels, peas, sliced artichokes, prawns and mushrooms. Mix in the lobster meat. Serve the paella piping hot.

GREEN PASTA AND TOMATO SAUCE
(TAGLIATELLE VERDI – ITALY)

Cooking time: 20 minutes

Serves 4

IMPERIAL · METRIC	AMERICAN
3 large onions	3 large onions
2 tablespoons olive oil	3 tablespoons olive oil
1 tablespoon tomato purée	1 tablespoon tomato paste
2 oz./50 g. grated Parmesan cheese	½ cup grated Parmesan cheese
¼ pint/1½ dl. red Cinzano	⅔ cup red Cinzano
1 6-oz./170-g. can tomatoes	1 6-oz. can tomatoes
2 cloves garlic	2 cloves garlic
1 bay leaf	1 bay leaf
1 1-lb./½-kg. packet green tagliatelle	1 1-lb. package green tagliatelle
2 oz./50 g. butter	¼ cup butter

Fry the chopped onions in the oil. Add the rest of the ingredients, except the pasta and butter, and simmer for 20 minutes. While the sauce is cooking, put the pasta into a large saucepan of boiling, salted water and cook gently for 20 minutes until tender. Drain and toss in the butter. Serve the sauce separately.

Various pizzas with Salade niçoise (pages 50 and 56)

49

RICE DISH

(PILAFF – GREECE)

Cooking time: 40 minutes
Oven temperature: 400°F., 200°C.,
Gas Mark 6

Serves 4

IMPERIAL · METRIC	AMERICAN
2 oz./50 g. butter	¼ cup butter
1 onion, chopped	1 onion, chopped
6 oz./175 g. long grain rice	scant 1 cup long grain rice
1 pint/6 dl. chicken stock	2½ cups chicken stock

Melt the butter and lightly fry the onion and rice until the butter has been absorbed.

Pour on the boiling stock and put into a casserole. Cover and cook near the bottom of a moderately hot oven for 30–35 minutes. Do not stir during cooking.

PIZZA

(ITALY)
Illustrated in colour on page 49

Cooking time: 20–30 minutes
Oven temperature: 450°F., 230°C.,
Gas Mark 8

Serves 6

IMPERIAL · METRIC	AMERICAN
1 lb./450 g. plain flour	4 cups all-purpose flour
2 level teaspoons salt	2 level teaspoons salt
½ oz./15 g. lard	1 tablespoon lard
about ¼ pint/1½ dl. water	about ⅔ cup water
oil	oil

Yeast liquid:
Dissolve ½ oz. (15 g., ½ cake compressed) fresh yeast in ¼ pint (1½ dl., ⅔ cup) water or dissolve 1 teaspoon sugar in ¼ pint (1½ dl., ⅔ cup) warm water and sprinkle 2 level teaspoons dried yeast on top. Stand aside for 10 minutes or until frothy.

Filling:	**Filling:**
1 lb./½ kg. Mozzarella or Cheddar cheese, grated	1 lb. Mozzarella or Cheddar cheese, grated
1 lb./½ kg. sliced fresh tomatoes or drained canned tomatoes	1 lb. sliced fresh tomatoes or drained canned tomatoes
pepper	pepper
1 teaspoon basil or thyme	1 teaspoon basil or thyme
Topping:	**Topping:**
anchovy fillets	anchovy fillets
capers (optional)	capers (optional)
black olives	ripe olives

Mix the flour and salt in a bowl and rub in the lard. Add the yeast liquid and sufficient water to make a soft dough. Knead the dough until it is smooth, firm and elastic and leaves the sides of the bowl clean. Shape the dough into a ball. Put to rise in a large greased polythene bag, loosely tied, or a large greased pan with a lid. Leave until the dough is double in size and springs back when pressed with a floured finger. It will take – 45–60 minutes in a warm place; 2 hours at room temperature; 12 hours in a cold room or larder.

Turn the risen dough on to a board and flatten with the knuckles or a rolling pin into a long strip. Brush with oil and roll up like a Swiss roll. Repeat this three times. Divide the dough into six pieces and roll each piece to a flat circle on a baking tin. Brush the dough with oil and cover with alternate layers of grated cheese, tomatoes and seasonings, finishing with cheese. Garnish with anchovies, capers and black olives. Bake for 20–30 minutes in a hot oven.

Salads and vegetable dishes

Crisp and green, savoury and succulent, a fresh salad can stand superbly on its own, or be served in place of vegetables. Salads can also be served as an extra vegetable with the main course.

To produce a really good salad it is essential to wash each ingredient with great care and then, most important, dry thoroughly. If time permits, chill the leaves also, and you'll make all the difference to the final result.

The best salads are served in a bowl (usually a wooden one), first rubbed with a garlic clove. The next job is to make your own dressing in the bowl, before the salad ingredients are added – don't be tempted to add the salad ingredients to the dressing until you're ready to serve the salad. Turn to page 75 to see how to make a French dressing.

GLOBE ARTICHOKES

This is a splendid vegetable, which deserves far more attention on this side of the Channel.

Cook the youngest ones in olive oil and lemon juice and with a few herbs, or cook them in dry white wine. Serve these artichokes as an hors d'oeuvre.

Try frying them, stuffing them and baking them. Serve with vinaigrette dressing, hollandaise sauce or melted butter.

And in case you don't know how to eat them – I didn't, I seriously thought I'd been presented with a table decoration! – then pull off each leaf separately and eat only the soft fleshy bit.

The hearts, or bases, are a true delicacy. They are found right at the base of the leaves. The 'choke' (stamens) must be discarded, but the hearts can be used for some wonderful hors d'oeuvre – the French, for example, top them with salmon and asparagus tips, or with mussels and lemon slices. Or the bases can simply be sliced in a delicious sauce.

RATATOUILLE

(FRANCE)

Cooking time: 40 minutes

Serves 4

IMPERIAL · METRIC	AMERICAN
1 green pepper	1 green sweet pepper
2 tablespoons olive oil	3 tablespoons olive oil
1 onion, sliced	1 onion, sliced
½ young marrow, peeled thinly and diced	½ young marrow squash, peeled thinly and diced
2 aubergines, thinly peeled and diced	2 eggplants, thinly peeled and diced
salt and pepper	salt and pepper
2 tomatoes, skinned and sliced	2 tomatoes, skinned and sliced
1 clove garlic, crushed	1 clove garlic, crushed
triangles of toast	triangles of toast

Split the green pepper in half, scoop out the seeds and discard. Shred the flesh fairly thinly. Heat the oil until very hot. Add the onion and the pepper, fry lightly until they are tender. Add the marrow and aubergine and continue cooking. Season with salt and pepper. Stir in the tomatoes and crushed garlic clove. Cover the pan. Simmer slowly for about 30 minutes, stirring occasionally. Serve piping hot, surrounded with triangles of toast.

COURGETTES IN TOMATO SAUCE

(COURGETTES À LA NIÇOISE – FRANCE)

Cooking time: 30 minutes

Serves 6

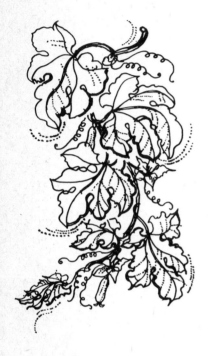

IMPERIAL · METRIC	AMERICAN
6 courgettes	6 small zucchini
2 oz./50 g. salt	scant ¼ cup salt
3 tablespoons olive oil	scant ¼ cup olive oil
Tomato sauce:	**Tomato sauce:**
(or use Quick tomato sauce, see page 77)	(or use Quick tomato sauce, see page 77)
1 oz./25 g. butter	2 tablespoons butter
1 rasher bacon	1 bacon slice
1 small onion, sliced	1 small onion, sliced
1 small carrot, sliced	1 small carrot, sliced
1 medium can tomatoes	1 medium can tomatoes
1 rounded teaspoon flour	1 rounded teaspoon flour
½ pint/3 dl. stock	1¼ cups stock
salt and pepper	salt and pepper
1 teaspoon sugar	1 teaspoon sugar
1 tablespoon vinegar	1 tablespoon vinegar
½ teaspoon thyme	½ teaspoon thyme
1 teaspoon dried tarragon	1 teaspoon dried tarragon
2 cloves garlic, crushed	2 cloves garlic, crushed
1 teaspoon lemon juice	1 teaspoon lemon juice

Cut the courgettes into ½-inch (1-cm.) slices. Sprinkle with salt and leave to drain for 30 minutes. Rinse and dry the courgettes in a teacloth. Fry in the olive oil until lightly brown and tender. Set aside and make the sauce.

Melt the butter in a pan, cut up the bacon and fry lightly. Add the sliced onion and carrot and fry without browning. Add the tomatoes to the ingredients in the pan. Cook for a few minutes. Add the flour, stock, seasoning, sugar, vinegar, thyme, half the tarragon, crushed garlic and lemon juice. Stir well and allow to simmer for 20 minutes. Rub through a wire sieve, adjust the seasoning and add the courgettes to the sauce. Sprinkle with the remaining tarragon. Serve well chilled with cold ham.

POTATOES WITH APPLES AND BACON

(KARTOFFELN MIT ÄPFELN UND SCHINKEN – GERMANY)

Cooking time: 25 minutes

Serves 4

IMPERIAL · METRIC	AMERICAN
1½ lb./¾ kg. potatoes	1½ lb. potatoes
1 lb./½ kg. apples	1 lb. apples
salt	salt
2 oz./50 g. sugar	¼ cup sugar
2 oz./50 g. bacon	3 bacon slices
1 oz./25 g. butter	2 tablespoons butter

Boil the potatoes. Mash them when cooked. Simmer the apples in the minimum of water, strain and pulp them. Thoroughly combine the potatoes and apples together, adding salt and sugar.

Fry the bacon in small pieces in the butter and pour over the potato and apple mixture before serving.

(Other fruits such as plums, prunes and pears can be used in a similar way.)

Apple strudel (page 66)

CAULIFLOWER AND CARROT SALAD

(SALADE JULIENNE – FRANCE)

Cooking time: 5 minutes

Serves 4

IMPERIAL · METRIC	AMERICAN
1 clove garlic	1 clove garlic
½ level teaspoon French mustard	½ level teaspoon French mustard
3 tablespoons olive oil	scant ¼ cup olive oil
1 tablespoon white wine vinegar	1 tablespoon white wine vinegar
½ level teaspoon salt	½ level teaspoon salt
½ level teaspoon pepper	½ level teaspoon pepper
4 oz./100 g. salami, sliced	¼ lb. salami, sliced
3 young carrots	3 young carrots
4 oz./100 g. tomatoes	¼ lb. tomatoes
1 small lettuce	1 small lettuce
1 small cauliflower	1 small cauliflower

Crush the garlic, add the mustard and blend with the oil. Gradually add the vinegar drop by drop, whisking well all the time. Season.
 Take the rind off the salami slices and cut the meat into thin strips. Scrape the carrots and cut into strips. Cut the tomatoes into wedges and wash and dry the lettuce. Wash the cauliflower in cold salted water and break into small pieces. Put the cauliflower pieces into a pan of boiling water for 5 minutes. Drain. Toss all the ingredients, one variety at a time, in the dressing. Serve on a bed of lettuce.

CHICORY – BELGIAN STYLE

(CHICORÉE PRÉPARÉE À LA BELGE – BELGIUM)

Cooking time: 1 hour 5 minutes
Oven temperature: 300°F., 150°C., Gas Mark 2

Serves 6

IMPERIAL · METRIC	AMERICAN
2 lb./1 kg. heads of chicory	2 lb. heads of Belgian endive
3 oz./75 g. butter, melted	6 tablespoons melted butter
pepper	pepper
meat extract (optional)	meat extract (optional)

Wash the chicory. Make a few cross cuts in the bottom of each head if thick. Put in a saucepan and cover with slightly salted, boiling water. Bring back to the boil. Boil for 5 minutes. Drain well. Turn into a casserole. Coat with melted butter. Season with pepper. Cover with a round of buttered paper, then with a lid.
 Simmer very gently, or bake in a cool oven for about 1 hour, turning once or twice. If liked, a few drops of meat extract can be added, to taste, when nearly ready.

MUSHROOMS IN TOMATO SAUCE

(CHAMPIGNONS PROVENÇALE – FRANCE)

Cooking time: 10 minutes

Serves 4–6

IMPERIAL · METRIC	AMERICAN
2 small cans mushrooms	2 small cans mushrooms
2 tablespoons olive oil	3 tablespoons olive oil
2 tablespoons tomato purée	3 tablespoons tomato paste
1 teaspoon lemon juice	1 teaspoon lemon juice
sprig of thyme	sprig of thyme
2–3 sprigs parsley	2–3 sprigs parsley
bay leaf	bay leaf
1 clove garlic, crushed	1 clove garlic, crushed
salt and pepper	salt and pepper

Place the mushrooms in a small frying pan with olive oil, tomato purée and lemon juice, thyme, the parsley sprigs, bay leaf, garlic, salt and pepper to taste. Stir and simmer for 1 minute. Cover and cook gently for 10 minutes. Remove the herbs. When cold, turn the mushrooms into an hors d'oeuvre dish.

HADDOCK, CUCUMBER AND TOMATO
(KOLJE, AGURK OG TOMAT-SALAT – NORWAY)

Cooking time: 50 minutes
Oven temperature: 400°F., 200°C., Gas Mark 6

Serves 4

IMPERIAL · METRIC	AMERICAN
1 large packet frozen haddock fillets	1 large package frozen haddock fillets
salt and pepper	salt and pepper
juice of 1 lemon	juice of 1 lemon
1 medium cucumber	1 medium cucumber
3 large tomatoes	3 large tomatoes
6 tablespoons wine vinegar	½ cup wine vinegar
1 heaped tablespoon castor sugar	1 heaped tablespoon sugar
finely chopped parsley	finely chopped parsley

Place the frozen haddock fillets in a greased heatproof dish. Season well and sprinkle with half the lemon juice. Bake for 50 minutes in the centre of a moderately hot oven. Drain and set aside to chill.

Meanwhile slice the cucumber and tomatoes thinly, sprinkle well with salt and remaining lemon juice. Chill well. Combine the vinegar and sugar, stirring until the sugar dissolves. Place the haddock on a serving dish. Arrange slices of cucumber and tomato attractively on top and spoon the vinegar mixture over. Sprinkle with chopped parsley and chill.

STUFFED CABBAGE LEAVES
(DOLMAS – GREECE)

Cooking time: 55 minutes

Serves 5

IMPERIAL · METRIC	AMERICAN
10 large cabbage leaves	10 large cabbage leaves
2 tablespoons olive oil	3 tablespoons olive oil
6 onions, chopped	6 onions, chopped
1 clove garlic, crushed	1 clove garlic, crushed
6 oz./175 g. long grain rice, cooked	scant 1 cup long grain rice, cooked
2 oz./50 g. sultanas	6 tablespoons seedless white raisins
6 tomatoes	6 tomatoes
shake grated nutmeg	shake grated nutmeg
salt and pepper	salt and pepper
tomato-flavoured gravy	tomato-flavored gravy

Wash the cabbage leaves and blanch them in boiling water for 1–2 minutes. Heat the oil in a pan. Add the chopped onions and the crushed garlic. Cook until just brown. Add the rice and the sultanas to the onions. Skin the tomatoes, after dipping them in boiling water, and chop. Add the chopped tomatoes to the rice mixture with the nutmeg, salt and pepper.

Remove a little of the thick cabbage stems and put tablespoons of the rice mixture on each leaf. Fold in the sides and roll up the leaves with the filling inside. Put them in a large pan and cover with salted water. Simmer for 45 minutes. Serve with tomato-flavoured gravy.

CAULIFLOWER SALAD

(SALADE DE CHOU-FLEUR –
FRANCE)

Cooking time: 10 minutes

Serves 4

IMPERIAL · METRIC	AMERICAN
1 medium cauliflower	1 medium cauliflower
French dressing	French dressing
paprika pepper	paprika pepper

Divide a firm white cauliflower into florets. Cook in boiling, salted water for 10 minutes. At once plunge into cold water. Drain, toss in French dressing and sprinkle with paprika pepper.

ARTICHOKES IN SAUCE (WITH BACON)

(ALCACHOFAS CON SALSA (CON JAMON) – SPAIN)

Cooking time: 15 minutes

Serves 4

IMPERIAL · METRIC	AMERICAN
1 medium onion	1 medium onion
1 clove garlic	1 clove garlic
sprig parsley	sprig parsley
2 oz./50 g. bacon, chopped	3 bacon slices, chopped
3 tablespoons olive oil or butter	scant $\frac{1}{4}$ cup olive oil or butter
$\frac{1}{4}$ pint/1$\frac{1}{2}$ dl. white wine	$\frac{2}{3}$ cup white wine
1 medium can artichokes	1 medium can artichokes
3 tablespoons stock	scant $\frac{1}{4}$ cup stock
salt and pepper	salt and pepper
paprika pepper	paprika pepper

Chop the onion, garlic and sprig of parsley. Place in a shallow saucepan with the bacon and olive oil or butter. Add the wine, drained artichokes, stock and season to taste. Cover. Simmer very gently for about 15 minutes.

LAYERED SALAD

(SALADE NIÇOISE – FRANCE)
Illustrated in colour on page 49

No cooking

Serves 4

IMPERIAL · METRIC	AMERICAN
1 lettuce	1 lettuce
3 tomatoes, quartered	3 tomatoes, quartered
1 red pepper, seeded and sliced	1 red sweet pepper, seeded and sliced
1 green pepper, seeded and sliced	1 green sweet pepper, seeded and sliced
8 black olives	8 ripe olives
2 sticks celery, sliced	2 stalks celery, sliced
1 medium can tuna fish or sardines	1 medium can tuna fish or sardines
6 anchovy fillets (optional)	6 anchovy fillets (optional)
3 hard-boiled eggs, sliced	3 hard-cooked eggs, sliced
Salad dressing:	**Salad dressing:**
6 tablespoons olive oil	$\frac{1}{2}$ cup olive oil
2 tablespoons tarragon vinegar	3 tablespoons tarragon vinegar
freshly ground black pepper	freshly ground black pepper
1 clove garlic, crushed	1 clove garlic, crushed

Break up and wash the lettuce, put in a salad bowl. Add the remaining ingredients, placing neatly on top the tuna fish, anchovies and sliced eggs. Blend all the salad dressing ingredients together just before serving and sprinkle over the salad.

Croissants (page 74)

POTATOES IN TOMATO STOCK

(BRÜHKARTOFFELN MIT TOMATEN – GERMANY)

Cooking time: 30 minutes

Serves 4

IMPERIAL · METRIC	AMERICAN
2 small onions, sliced	2 small onions, sliced
1 oz./25 g. butter	2 tablespoons butter
8 oz./225 g. tomatoes or 1 8-oz./ 225-g. can tomatoes	½ lb. tomatoes or 1 8-oz. can tomatoes
generous ½ pint/3 dl. stock	generous 1¼ cups stock
salt and pepper	salt and pepper
1½ lb./¾ kg. potatoes	1½ lb. potatoes
1 tablespoon chopped parsley	1 tablespoon chopped parsley

Cook the onions in butter, then add the peeled and seeded tomatoes, roughly cut up. Add the stock and seasoning. Boil the potatoes in their jackets for 10 minutes. Peel, slice thickly and cook until tender in the tomato stock. Sprinkle with chopped parsley.

SALAD WITH POLISH SOUR CREAM DRESSING

(SALAT PO POLSKU ZE SMIETANA – POLAND)

No cooking

Serves 6

IMPERIAL · METRIC	AMERICAN
3 hard-boiled eggs	3 hard-cooked eggs
¼ pint/1½ dl. soured cream	⅔ cup sour cream
½ teaspoon sugar (optional)	½ teaspoon sugar (optional)
lemon juice or white vinegar to taste	lemon juice or white vinegar to taste
salt and pepper	salt and pepper
green salad to serve	green salad to serve

Cream 2 egg yolks with the soured cream. Add sugar if wished, lemon juice or white vinegar, and salt and pepper to taste; stir thoroughly. Add to the green salad. Chop the remaining egg whites and use for garnish, together with the third egg, cut into thin slices.

FRIED POTATO STRIPS

(RÖSTI – SWITZERLAND)

Cooking time: 25 minutes

Serves 4

IMPERIAL · METRIC	AMERICAN
2 lb./1 kg. King Edward or Majestic potatoes	2 lb. potatoes
4 oz./100 g. butter	½ cup butter

Wash but do not peel the potatoes. Boil in salted water until tender, but firm. Leave until cold. Peel and cut the potatoes into strips, about ¾ inch (1·5 cm.) wide (or you can grate them if you prefer). Heat the butter and fry the potato strips until golden brown on both sides, shaping the mixture to a round. Turn on to a hot plate and serve.

Variations

a Add 2 tablespoons (U.S. 3 tablespoons) chopped onion to the pan before cooking.

b Add 2 oz. (50 g.) diced bacon.

c Grate Emmenthal cheese over the potatoes just before they are cooked.

Puddings and sweets

CREAM MOULD WITH MORELLO SAUCE

(FLØDERAND MET KIRSEBAER SOVS – DENMARK)

Cooking time: 10 minutes

Serves 4–5

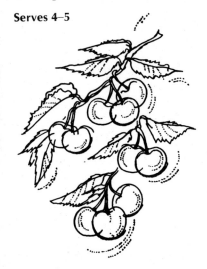

We have grown up with milk and steamed puddings, so that it is hard to realise that they scarcely exist across the Channel where so often a meal is brought to its conclusion with fresh fruit.

There are, however, some gorgeous Continental recipes for open tarts, mouth-watering ices and a number of wonderful fruit desserts. The French specialise in delicious soufflés and creams that are very easy to make.

IMPERIAL · METRIC	AMERICAN
2 egg yolks	2 egg yolks
1 oz./25 g. sugar	2 tablespoons sugar
3 tablespoons Madeira or sherry	scant ¼ cup Madeira or sherry
3 level teaspoons powdered gelatine	4 level teaspoons powdered gelatin
2–3 tablespoons hot water	3–4 tablespoons hot water
2 6-oz./170-g. cans cream	2 6-oz. cans cream
2 oz./50 g. almonds, blanched and chopped	½ cup blanched and chopped almonds
Morello sauce:	**Morello sauce:**
1 8-oz./226-g. can Morello cherries	1 8-oz. can Morello cherries
3 tablespoons water	scant ¼ cup water
1 level tablespoon cornflour	1 level tablespoon cornstarch
cold water to mix	cold water to mix

Whisk the egg yolks with the sugar until the mixture is light and creamy. Add the Madeira and whisk. Dissolve gelatine in the water, cool and add to the egg mixture. Beat the cream well; add the almonds and fold the cream into egg mixture. Pour into a 1-pint (6-dl., 2½-cup) mould, which has been rinsed in cold water and sprinkled on the inside with a little sugar. Leave until set then turn out.

To make the Morello sauce, empty the can of cherries into a saucepan, add the water and bring to the boil. Dissolve the cornflour in a little cold water and add to cherries. Boil for 2 minutes. Serve the cream mould with the *hot* Morello sauce.

ZABAGLIONE

(ITALY)
Illustrated on the jacket

Cooking time: 15 minutes

Serves 3

IMPERIAL · METRIC	AMERICAN
2 oz./50 g. sugar	¼ cup sugar
1 tablespoon water	1 tablespoon water
1 egg white	1 egg white
3 egg yolks	3 egg yolks
1 tablespoon Marsala	1 tablespoon Marsala

Put the sugar and water into a small pan and when sugar has dissolved, boil quickly until it will draw a thread between two spoons. Beat the egg white until stiff, add the sugar syrup and mix quickly with a whisk. Place the yolks and Marsala in a basin and whisk over hot water until thick and mousse-like, being careful not to overheat the eggs. Combine Marsala mixture with meringue mixture and pour into glasses. Chill.

CHOCOLATE CUPS

(PETITS POTS DE CRÈME – FRANCE)

Cooking time: 15 minutes

Serves 4

IMPERIAL · METRIC	AMERICAN
1 small can evaporated milk	1 small can evaporated milk
½ teaspoon vanilla essence	½ teaspoon vanilla extract
2 level tablespoons cornflour	3 level tablespoons cornstarch
1 level tablespoon castor sugar	1 level tablespoon sugar
4 oz./100 g. plain chocolate	4 squares semi-sweet chocolate
1 egg yolk	1 egg yolk
1 oz./25 g. butter, softened	2 tablespoons softened butter

Make the evaporated milk up to ¾ pint (4 dl., scant 2 cups) with water. Add the vanilla essence. Mix the cornflour and sugar to a smooth paste with about 2 tablespoons of the milk, and put the remainder of the milk on to heat. Just before it reaches boiling point, pour the milk into the cornflour mixture, stirring well. Return to a clean saucepan, bring to the boil, stirring, and cook for 3 minutes.

Meanwhile, melt the chocolate in a bowl over hot water and add to the milk and cornflour with the egg yolk. Beat well until smooth. Cool for 10 minutes and add the butter gradually, beating well. Pile into individual dessert cups or glasses, chill and serve.

If liked, the chocolate cups may be topped with a chocolate curl or piped with cream just before serving.

FRUIT DUMPLINGS

(OVOCNÉ KNEDLÍKY – CZECHOSLOVAKIA)

Cooking time: 10 minutes

Serves 4

IMPERIAL · METRIC	AMERICAN
8 oz./225 g. boiled potatoes	½ lb. boiled potatoes
2 oz./50 g. butter	¼ cup butter
5 oz./150 g. plain flour	1¼ cups all-purpose flour
⅛ teaspoon salt	⅛ teaspoon salt
1 small egg, beaten	1 egg, beaten
16 plums, apricots or large prunes	16 plums, apricots or large prunes
16 lumps of sugar	16 lumps of sugar
little brandy (optional)	little brandy (optional)
2 oz./50 g. castor sugar	¼ cup sugar
3 oz./75 g. fine white breadcrumbs or rusk crumbs	1½ cups fine white bread crumbs or rusk crumbs

Sieve the potato, while still warm, into a basin. Beat in ½ oz. (15 g., 1 tablespoon) of the butter, then sift in the flour and salt and lastly the egg. Knead to a smooth dough. Roll out thinly and cut into squares.

Remove the stones from the fruit and insert a small lump of sugar, sprinkled with brandy if liked. Place a fruit on each square. Sprinkle with castor sugar, reserving some for later use, then wrap round with the dough. Cut off any extra dough, smooth the edges together well and roll lightly into balls.

Drop into a large pan of boiling water, cover and simmer gently for 10 minutes. Drain. Meanwhile, melt the remaining butter and gently fry the breadcrumbs until golden. Roll the dumplings in the crumbs and serve sprinkled with castor sugar.

Danish apple dessert (page 67)

ORANGE WHIP

(KONG HAKON PARFAIT
(APPELSIN-FROMASJ) – NORWAY)

No cooking

Serves 4

IMPERIAL · METRIC	AMERICAN
4 oranges	4 oranges
4 oz./100 g. castor sugar	½ cup sugar
1 pint/6 dl. double cream	2½ cups heavy cream
4 egg yolks, well-beaten	4 egg yolks, well-beaten

Cut off the tops from the oranges. Scoop out the flesh of three oranges carefully, and chop. Squeeze out the juice of the remaining orange. Whisk the sugar and cream until stiff, then add the egg yolks and orange juice. Stir in the chopped segments.

Fill the oranges with the mixture and replace the tops as lids. Chill well until ready to serve.

PROFITEROLES

(FRANCE)

Cooking time: 55 minutes
Oven temperature: 375° F., 190° C.,
Gas Mark 5

Serves 4

IMPERIAL · METRIC	AMERICAN
Choux pastry:	**Choux pastry:**
2 oz./50 g. butter	¼ cup butter
¼ pint/1½ dl. water	⅔ cup water
2½ oz./60 g. plain flour	½ cup and 2 tablespoons all-purpose flour
pinch salt	pinch salt
2 large eggs	2 eggs
Pastry cream:	**Pastry cream:**
1 egg and 1 yolk	1 egg and 1 yolk
2 oz./50 g. castor sugar	¼ cup sugar
1 oz./25 g. flour	¼ cup all-purpose flour
½ pint/3 dl. milk	1¼ cups milk
vanilla essence	vanilla extract
1 oz./25 g. butter	2 tablespoons butter
Chocolate sauce:	**Chocolate sauce:**
1 pint/6 dl. water	2½ cups water
4 oz./100 g. plain chocolate	4 squares semi-sweet chocolate
4 level tablespoons sugar	5 level tablespoons sugar
½ level tablespoon cocoa powder	½ level tablespoon unsweetened cocoa powder
1 level teaspoon instant coffee powder	1 level teaspoon instant coffee powder
1 teaspoon vanilla essence	1 teaspoon vanilla extract

Put the butter and water into a pan and bring to the boil. Sieve the flour and salt on to paper and tip into the pan all at once. Remove from the heat and beat until the paste is smooth and will leave the sides of the pan. Cool slightly. Whisk the eggs lightly and very gradually add to the paste, beating thoroughly.

Put teaspoonfuls of the mixture on to damp baking trays and bake in a moderately hot oven for 25–30 minutes. Cool on a wire tray and then split round the base.

To make the pastry cream, mix together the eggs, sugar and flour. Warm the milk and pour on to the eggs. Return to the pan and bring to the boil, stirring continuously. Remove from the heat, add a little essence and beat in the butter. Cool. Using a large fluted tube, pipe a little into each case, or use a teaspoon. Pile the choux buns on a glass dish.

To make the sauce, put all the ingredients except the vanilla into a pan and bring slowly to the boil. Stir until the sugar has dissolved and then simmer for about 20 minutes until the sauce looks 'syrupy'. Add the vanilla essence and pour over the profiteroles.

SPICED APPLE TART
(APPELTAART – HOLLAND)

Cooking time: 45 minutes
Oven temperatures: 425°F., 220°C.,
Gas Mark 7; 350° F., 180° C.,
Gas Mark 4

Serves 6

IMPERIAL · METRIC	AMERICAN
4 oz./100 g. butter	$\frac{1}{2}$ cup butter
8 oz./225 g. plain flour	2 cups all-purpose flour
water to mix	water to mix
1 lb./$\frac{1}{2}$ kg. apples, peeled and cored	1 lb. apples, peeled and cored
4 oz./100 g. brown sugar	$\frac{1}{2}$ cup brown sugar
2 oz./50 g. sultanas	scant $\frac{1}{2}$ cup seedless white raisins
1 level teaspoon cinnamon	1 level teaspoon cinnamon
grated rind of $\frac{1}{2}$ lemon	grated rind of $\frac{1}{2}$ lemon
1 tablespoon icing sugar	1 tablespoon confectioners' sugar
fresh cream to serve	fresh cream to serve

Make the pastry by rubbing the butter into the sieved flour and mixing to a stiff dough with water. Roll out and line an 8-inch (20-cm.) sandwich tin with the pastry. Cut a round to form a lid. Slice the apples and mix with the sugar, sultanas, cinnamon and lemon rind. Spread this mixture over pastry and cover with a lid. Mark round the edge of the tart to decorate. Make a few holes in the top and bake on the centre shelf of a hot oven, 425°F., 220°C., Gas Mark 7, for 10–15 minutes, then a further 30 minutes at moderate, 350°F., 180°C., Gas Mark 4. Sprinkle icing sugar over the top and serve with cream.

APPLE AND CREAM CRUMBLE
(TILSLORTE BONDEPIKER – NORWAY)

No cooking

Serves 4

IMPERIAL · METRIC	AMERICAN
2 oz./50 g. cake crumbs	1 cup cake crumbs
6 oz./175 g. stewed apples, drained	$\frac{3}{4}$ cup drained, stewed apples
$\frac{1}{4}$–$\frac{1}{2}$ pint/1$\frac{1}{2}$–3 dl. whipped cream	$\frac{2}{3}$ cup–1$\frac{1}{4}$ cups whipped cream

Place a thin layer of cake crumbs in a serving dish, then a layer of apples and a layer of cream. Repeat layers, decorating the top with cream. Chill until ready to serve.

CREAM AND JAM DESSERT
(GRÄDDTÄRTA – SWEDEN)

No cooking

Serves 4

IMPERIAL · METRIC	AMERICAN
$\frac{1}{2}$ pint/3 dl. double cream	1$\frac{1}{4}$ cups whipping cream
4 oz./100 g. jam	scant $\frac{1}{2}$ cup jam or jelly
8 oz./225 g. broken biscuits	$\frac{1}{2}$ lb. broken cookies

Whip the cream. Spread jam on the broken biscuits. Fill a serving bowl with alternate layers of cream and jam-spread biscuits, finishing with a layer of cream. Decorate the top with piped jam.

ORANGE CREAM

(SABAYON DE NARANJA – SPAIN)

Cooking time: 10–15 minutes

Serves 6

IMPERIAL · METRIC	AMERICAN
4 egg yolks	4 egg yolks
2 oz./50 g. sugar	$\frac{1}{4}$ cup sugar
juice of $\frac{1}{2}$ lemon	juice of $\frac{1}{2}$ lemon
2 tablespoons orange squash	3 tablespoons undiluted orange drink
$\frac{1}{2}$ pint/3 dl. orange juice	$1\frac{1}{4}$ cups orange juice
2 tablespoons sherry (optional)	3 tablespoons sherry (optional)
1 egg	1 egg
$\frac{1}{2}$ pint/3 dl. milk	$1\frac{1}{4}$ cups milk

Whisk the egg yolks, sugar, lemon, orange squash, orange juice and sherry, if used, together in a double saucepan over a low heat until light and fluffy. Whisk the egg and milk together and add to the mixture. Continue whisking until thick and frothy. Serve in individual glasses.

PEAR SAVARIN

(SAVARIN DE POIRES – FRANCE)

Cooking time: 35 minutes
Oven temperatures: 400°F., 200°C.,
Gas Mark 6; 350°F., 180°C.,
Gas Mark 4

Serves 8

IMPERIAL · METRIC	AMERICAN
8 oz./225 g. plain flour	2 cups all-purpose flour
2 level teaspoons fresh yeast	scant $\frac{1}{2}$ cake compressed yeast
3 tablespoons warm milk	scant $\frac{1}{4}$ cup warm milk
4 eggs	4 eggs
6 oz./175 g. butter	$\frac{3}{4}$ cup butter
$\frac{1}{2}$ teaspoon salt	$\frac{1}{2}$ teaspoon salt
$\frac{1}{2}$ oz./15 g. sugar	1 tablespoon sugar
1 pear, peeled, cored and chopped	1 pear, peeled, cored and chopped
Syrup:	**Syrup:**
6–12 tablespoons water	$\frac{1}{2}$–1 cup water
4–8 tablespoons sugar	5–10 tablespoons sugar
1–2 tablespoons rum	1–2 tablespoons rum
Glaze:	**Glaze:**
6 oz./175 g. apricot jam, warmed and sieved	about $\frac{1}{2}$ cup apricot jam or jelly, warmed and sieved
4 pears, peeled, cored and halved	4 pears, peeled, cored and halved
juice of 1 lemon	juice of 1 lemon

Sieve the flour into a warmed bowl. Make a well in the centre and add the yeast, milk and eggs. Mix by hand for a few minutes until evenly blended. Dot the surface with small pieces of softened butter, then cover the bowl and put in a warm place until the mixture doubles in size. Add salt and sugar and beat thoroughly until mixture begins to stiffen, approximately 5–8 minutes. (Alternatively use the dough hook of an electric mixer.) Stir in the chopped pear. Put the mixture into a large greased savarin mould – the mould should not be more than half full. Prove until mixture is level with top of the mould.
  Bake in the centre of a moderately hot oven (400°F., 200°C., Gas Mark 6) for 10 minutes and then reduce heat to moderate (350°F., 180°C., Gas Mark 4) for a further 20–25 minutes.
  Meanwhile dissolve the water, sugar and rum in a small saucepan, bring to the boil and simmer to form a light syrup. Unmould the savarin whilst hot and immediately marinate with the warm syrup. When cool,

spoon or brush over half the apricot glaze for a shiny finish.
Brush the pear halves with lemon juice and coat with remaining apricot glaze – if the pears are under-ripe, poach lightly before using. Serve them separately.

ORANGE PANCAKES
(CRÈPES SUZETTE – FRANCE)

Cooking time: 10 minutes

Makes about 12

IMPERIAL · METRIC	AMERICAN
Orange butter:	**Orange butter:**
3 lumps of sugar	*3 lumps of sugar*
1 orange	*1 orange*
1½ oz./40 g. butter	*3 tablespoons butter*
1 oz./25 g. castor sugar	*2 tablespoons sugar*
1 tablespoon orange juice	*1 tablespoon orange juice*
1 tablespoon orange Curaçao	*1 tablespoon orange Curaçao*
Batter:	**Batter:**
4½ oz./110 g. plain flour	*1 cup plus 2 tablespoons all-purpose flour*
pinch salt	*pinch salt*
1¾ oz./40 g. sugar	*3½ tablespoons sugar*
2 large eggs	*2 eggs*
½ pint/3 dl. boiled milk, cold	*1¼ cups boiled milk, cold*
1 tablespoon melted butter	*1 tablespoon melted butter*
1 tablespoon orange juice	*1 tablespoon orange juice*
3–4 tablespoons rum or brandy	*4–5 tablespoons rum or brandy*

Rub the lumps of sugar over the orange rind until they have absorbed the oil of the orange. Crush the sugar lumps and beat into the butter. Add the castor sugar, orange juice and Curaçao.

Sift the flour and salt for the batter into a bowl, add the sugar. Make a well in the flour and break in the eggs. Add a little of the milk. Blend the eggs and milk together and then work in the flour. Beat well. Add melted butter and the rest of the milk. Leave to rest for 1½ hours.

Mix in the orange juice and 1 tablespoon of rum or brandy. Grease a small frying pan with a very little butter and cook the pancakes until lightly browned. They should be paper thin.

When all the pancakes are made, reheat in a chafing dish, the oven or a large frying pan. Spoon over the orange butter. Heat the remaining rum or brandy, ignite it and pour over the pancakes. Serve piping hot.

ICE CREAM CURAÇAO
(CRÈME CURAÇAO – FRANCE)

No cooking

Serves 6

IMPERIAL · METRIC	AMERICAN
¼ pint/1½ dl. double cream	*⅔ cup whipping cream*
1–1½ tablespoons Curaçao	*1½–2 tablespoons Curaçao*
1 family brick dairy ice cream	*1 quart ice cream*
1 stick cinnamon	*1 stick cinnamon*
sponge fingers or ice cream wafers	*ladyfingers or ice cream wafers*

Whip the cream until fairly thick. Fold in the Curaçao. Cut the block of dairy ice cream into small cubes and divide these equally between 6 glass bowls. Break the cinnamon stick into small flakes and sprinkle these over the ice cream cubes. Top each portion with a whirl of the Curaçao-flavoured cream. Serve with sponge fingers or ice cream wafers.

LEMON SOUFFLÉ

(SOUFFLÉ AUX CITRONS – FRANCE)

Cooking time: 10 minutes

Serves 4

IMPERIAL · METRIC	AMERICAN
$\frac{1}{4}$ pint/1$\frac{1}{2}$ dl. double cream	$\frac{2}{3}$ cup whipping cream
$\frac{1}{2}$ oz./15 g. gelatine	2 envelopes gelatin
3 tablespoons water	scant $\frac{1}{4}$ cup water
3 standard eggs	3 eggs
3 oz./75 g. castor sugar	6 tablespoons sugar
grated rind and juice of 2 lemons	grated rind and juice of 2 lemons
chopped nuts for decoration	chopped nuts for decoration
whipped cream	whipped cream

Tie a double band of greaseproof paper firmly round a 1-pint ($\frac{1}{2}$-litre, 2$\frac{1}{2}$-cup) soufflé dish so that 3 inches (7·5 cm.) of paper stand above the rim. Lightly whip the cream. Dissolve the gelatine in the water in a small pan. Separate the eggs. Whisk the yolks, sugar, lemon rind and juice in a basin over a saucepan of hot water until thick and creamy. Do not let the water boil or the basin touch the water. Remove from the heat and continue whisking until cold.

When almost set, pour the gelatine in a thin stream on to the mixture, whisking all the time.

Whisk the egg whites until stiff. Fold in the cream and egg whites. Pour into the prepared soufflé dish. Leave to set. Remove the paper carefully with a knife dipped in hot water. Coat the sides of the soufflé with chopped nuts and decorate with whipped cream.

APPLE STRUDEL

(AUSTRIA)

Illustrated in colour on page 53

Cooking time: 40 minutes
Oven temperature: 375° F., 190° C., Gas Mark 5

Serves 6

IMPERIAL · METRIC	AMERICAN
8 oz./225 g. plain flour	2 cups all-purpose flour
1 level teaspoon salt	1 level teaspoon salt
1 egg	1 egg
2 oz./50 g. butter, melted	$\frac{1}{4}$ cup butter, melted
4 tablespoons water	scant $\frac{1}{2}$ cup water
Filling:	**Filling:**
2 lb./1 kg. cooking apples	2 lb. baking apples
2 oz./50 g. soft white breadcrumbs	1 cup soft white bread crumbs
4 oz./100 g. sultanas	$\frac{3}{4}$ cup seedless white raisins
2 oz./50 g. ground almonds	$\frac{1}{2}$ cup ground almonds
4 oz./100 g. brown sugar	$\frac{1}{2}$ cup brown sugar
$\frac{1}{2}$ tablespoon mixed spice	$\frac{1}{2}$ tablespoon mixed spice
1 lemon	1 lemon
2 oz./50 g. butter, melted	$\frac{1}{4}$ cup butter, melted
1 oz./25 g. icing sugar	$\frac{1}{4}$ cup confectioners' sugar
whipped cream to serve	whipped cream to serve

Sieve the flour and salt into a ring on a smooth surface. Break the egg into the centre of the ring. Add 1 oz. (25 g., 2 tablespoons) of the melted butter and the water which has been warmed. Work the flour gradually into the liquid with the fingers, working in a circular movement. Knead lightly until the paste is smooth and soft; put aside and leave for 20 minutes.

Peel and core the apples and slice them. Mix with the breadcrumbs, sultanas, ground almonds, brown sugar, mixed spice and grated lemon rind and juice. Roll out the strudel paste to an 8-inch (20-cm.) square and brush lightly with some of the melted butter. Put on a floured cloth; pull gently with backs of the hands under the paste, until paper thin. Brush with more butter; scatter the apple mixture over. Roll up the strudel very carefully with the aid of the cloth. Curve into a horseshoe shape and slide gently on to a greased baking tin. Brush with the remaining melted butter.

Bake on the centre shelf of a moderate oven, for 40 minutes, until golden. Dredge the top with icing sugar. Serve in slices, accompanied by whipped cream.

PEARS IN BRANDY

(POIRES FLAMBÉES – FRANCE)

No cooking

IMPERIAL · METRIC	AMERICAN
halved and peeled pears	*halved and peeled pears*
icing sugar	*confectioners' sugar*
1 tablespoon warmed brandy to each pear half	*1 tablespoon warmed brandy to each pear half*

Sprinkle the pear halves with icing sugar and pour brandy over each one. Ignite at the table.

DANISH APPLE DESSERT

(GAMMELDAGS AEBLE – DENMARK)
Illustrated in colour on page 61

Cooking time: 15 minutes

Serves 4

IMPERIAL · METRIC	AMERICAN
1½ lb./¾ kg. cooking apples	1½ lb. baking apples
2½ oz./65 g. butter	5 tablespoons butter
sugar to sweeten	sugar to sweeten
lemon rind to flavour	lemon rind to flavor
5 oz./150 g. coarse soft white breadcrumbs	2½ cups coarse soft white bread crumbs
whipped cream	whipped cream
1 red-skinned apple, sliced	1 red-skinned apple, sliced
few maraschino cherries	few maraschino cherries
grated chocolate	grated chocolate

Peel, core and slice the apples. Rub a saucepan round with ½ oz. (15 g., 1 tablespoon) butter, put in the apples with sufficient sugar to sweeten and a little grated lemon rind. Cover and simmer until soft.

Meanwhile dry the breadcrumbs slightly in the oven, melt the remaining butter in a frying pan. Fry the crumbs to a golden brown colour. Fill glasses with alternate layers of apple and crumbs until nearly full. Top with whipped cream. Garnish with slices of apple and a cherry, then sprinkle with grated chocolate.

Cakes, biscuits and pastries

Even if we have never been abroad, we all know how clever Continental cooks are when baking pastries – just remember those calorie-laden copies in coffee bars! The real thing tends to be even bigger and more eye-catching, but it's not so difficult to make them yourself and win great admiration from your family and friends.

PUFF PASTRY GÂTEAU

(GÂTEAU PITHIVIERS – FRANCE)

Cooking time: 25 minutes
Oven temperature: 450°F., 230°C.,
Gas Mark 8

IMPERIAL · METRIC	AMERICAN
1 oz./25 g. unsalted butter	2 tablespoons sweet butter
1 oz./25 g. castor sugar	2 tablespoons sugar
1 egg yolk	1 egg yolk
1 oz./25 g. ground almonds	$\frac{1}{4}$ cup ground almonds
few drops vanilla essence	few drops vanilla extract
8 oz./225 g. puff pastry	$\frac{1}{2}$ lb. puff paste
apricot jam	apricot jam or jelly
icing sugar	confectioners' sugar

Cream the butter. Then add the sugar and beat very thoroughly. Work in most of the egg yolk gradually (leaving enough to brush over the pastry later); fold in the ground almonds and the flavouring. Roll out the puff pastry to $\frac{3}{8}$ inch (0·5 cm.) thick and cut 2 circles about the size of a dessert plate. Put one piece of pastry on to a wetted baking sheet and cover liberally to within 1½ inches (3·5 cm.) of the edge with apricot jam. Put the almond filling in the centre, dome-shaped. Damp the pastry edges. Arrange the second piece of pastry over the top, pressing firmly round the edges and sealing well. Make three or four cuts in the top with a sharp knife. Brush over with the rest of the egg yolk and mark in a cartwheel design. Sprinkle with icing sugar.

   Bake for 25 minutes on the second shelf of a hot oven. Serve cold.

OLD-FASHIONED HONEYCAKE

(GAMMELDAGS HONNINGKAGE – DENMARK)

Cooking time: 1 hour
Oven temperature: 350°F., 180°C.,
Gas Mark 4

IMPERIAL · METRIC	AMERICAN
10 oz./275 g. butter	1¼ cups butter
13 oz./375 g. clear honey	generous 1 cup clear honey
6 eggs	6 eggs
3 oz./75 g. castor sugar	6 tablespoons sugar
1 lb./450 g. plain flour	1 lb. all-purpose flour
2 level teaspoons baking powder	2 level teaspoons baking powder
1 level teaspoon ground ginger	1 level teaspoon ground ginger
1 level teaspoon ground cloves	1 level teaspoon ground cloves
glacé icing (see page 77)	glacé icing (see page 77)
glacé cherries	candied cherries
hazelnuts to decorate	hazelnuts to decorate

Cream the butter well. Beat to a smooth consistency with the honey. Beat the eggs together, then beat gradually into the butter and honey. Add the sugar and beat until the mixture is light. Sieve the flour, baking powder and spices together, fold into the butter mixture. Bake in a greased oblong tin, approximately 9 inches by 11 inches (23 cm. × 28 cm.), in the centre of a moderate oven. Cool on a wire rack.

   Decorate with glacé icing, cherries and hazelnuts. Store for 2–3 weeks.

CREAM CHEESE GÂTEAU

(FLØDEOST – LAGKAGE –
DENMARK)

Cooking time: 25 minutes
Oven temperature: 400°F., 200°C.,
Gas Mark 6

Serves 6

IMPERIAL · METRIC	AMERICAN
8 oz./225 g. butter, chilled	1 cup butter, chilled
8 oz./225 g. plain flour	2 cups all-purpose flour
½ teaspoon salt	½ teaspoon salt
3 tablespoons single cream	scant ¼ cup coffee cream
2–4 oz./50–100 g. cream cheese	¼–½ cup cream cheese
¼ pint/1½ dl. double cream	⅔ cup whipping cream
2 fresh or canned peaches, sliced	2 fresh or canned peaches, sliced

Rub the butter into the flour and salt. Mix into a dough with the cream. Wrap in foil or greaseproof paper and leave in a cold place for 1 hour. Roll out the dough and line a 7-inch (18-cm.) flan ring. Prick the base and fill with a piece of greaseproof paper and some haricot beans or dry crusts.

Bake in the centre of a moderately hot oven for 25 minutes. Turn out on to a wire rack and leave to cool. Beat the cheese until soft; add the cream. Place the sliced peaches in the base of the cold flan case and pile the cream cheese mixture on top.

GINGER SHORTBREAD

(GEMBER BOTERKOEK – HOLLAND)

Cooking time: 30 minutes
Oven temperature: 350°F., 180°C.,
Gas Mark 4

IMPERIAL · METRIC	AMERICAN
7 oz./200 g. butter	generous ¾ cup butter
9 oz./250 g. plain flour, sieved	2¼ cups sifted all-purpose flour
pinch salt	pinch salt
7 oz./200 g. castor sugar	generous ¾ cup sugar
3 oz./75 g. preserved ginger, finely chopped	⅓ cup finely chopped preserved ginger
1 egg, beaten (reserve a little for glazing)	1 egg, beaten (reserve a little for glazing)

Knead all the ingredients together to form a smooth dough. Press into an 8-inch (20-cm.) cake tin and flatten the top. Glaze with beaten egg and mark with a fork.

Cook on the middle shelf of a moderate oven for 30 minutes. While still hot, press down the centre with the back of a spoon or clean oven cloth. Leave to cool and cut into slices.

BUTTER BISCUITS

(BOTERMOPPEN – HOLLAND)

Cooking time: about 20 minutes
Oven temperature: 375°F., 190°C.,
Gas Mark 5

Makes about 30

IMPERIAL · METRIC	AMERICAN
6 oz./175 g. butter	¾ cup butter
5 oz./150 g. sugar	½ cup plus 2 tablespoons sugar
few drops vanilla essence	few drops vanilla extract
8 oz./225 g. plain flour	2 cups all-purpose flour

Cream the butter and sugar, add the essence. Stir in the flour. Sprinkle a board with granulated sugar and roll the mixture into a sausage shape. Cool, using a refrigerator if possible, until the mixture is really firm. Cut into slices, place on a baking sheet and bake in the centre of a moderately hot oven for about 20 minutes until pale brown at the edges.

CHOCOLATE CREAM FILLED FINGERS

(LINZERSCHNITTEN – AUSTRIA)

Cooking time: 10 minutes
Oven temperature: 375°F., 190°C.,
Gas Mark 5

Serves 6

IMPERIAL · METRIC
Pastry:
9 oz./250 g. plain flour
9 oz./250 g. castor sugar
7 oz./200 g. butter
1 egg yolk
lemon juice and rind of ½ lemon
icing sugar
Filling:
¼ pint/1½ dl. double cream
1½ oz./40 g. sugar
2 oz./50 g. chocolate, grated

AMERICAN
Pastry:
2¼ cups all-purpose flour
1 cup plus 2 tablespoons sugar
¾ cup plus 2 tablespoons butter
1 egg yolk
lemon juice and rind of ½ lemon
confectioners' sugar
Filling:
⅔ cup whipping cream
3 tablespoons sugar
scant ½ cup grated chocolate

Sift together the flour and sugar, then rub in the butter until the mixture resembles fine breadcrumbs. Add the egg yolk and lemon juice and rind and mix well with a fork. Knead to a smooth dough. If easier, divide the dough for rolling out. Roll out to a rectangle ¼ inch (0·5 cm.) thick. Bake on buttered and floured baking sheets in a moderately hot oven for 10 minutes. Trim off crisp edges and cut into slices while still warm. Whip the cream until stiff, fold in the sugar. Set aside a little of the whipped cream for decoration.

Fold the grated chocolate into the larger amount of cream and spread half the slices with this. Top with remaining slices and decorate with the rest of the whipped cream. Dust with icing sugar.

Fill just before serving. Store in an airtight container, unfilled.

ALMOND PASTRIES

(LOUKOUMIAH – CYPRUS)

Cooking time: 15 minutes
Oven temperature: 400°F., 200°C.,
Gas Mark 6

IMPERIAL · METRIC
1 lb./450 g. fine semolina
6 oz./175 g. butter
warm water
Filling:
8 oz./225 g. ground almonds
4 oz./100 g. almonds, chopped
4 oz./100 g. sugar
orange flower water or grated
   orange rind and juice
Topping:
4 oz./100 g. icing sugar
orange flower water or juice to mix
2 oz./50 g. chopped almonds or
   candied orange peel

AMERICAN
2⅔ cups fine semolina flour
¾ cup butter
warm water
Filling:
2 cups ground almonds
1 cup chopped almonds
½ cup sugar
orange flower water or grated
   orange rind and juice
Topping:
scant 1 cup confectioners' sugar
orange flower water or juice to mix
½ cup chopped almonds or candied
   orange peel

Stir the semolina into the melted butter, mixing well. Leave overnight. Stir in just enough warm water to mix to a pliable dough. Break off small pieces and press into oval shapes, large enough to hold about 1 tablespoon of filling (or roll and cut into rounds).

Mix the ground almonds, chopped almonds and sugar, and mix into a paste with the orange flower water (or with grated rind and orange juice).

Fill the pastry shapes, moistening the edges and pinching together.

Bake in the centre of a moderately hot oven for about 15 minutes. When cold, top with orange flavoured glacé icing and sprinkle with chopped almonds or candied peel.

FRUIT AND NUT BISCUITS
(MOR MONSEN – NORWAY)

Cooking time: 30–40 minutes
Oven temperature: 375°F., 190°C., Gas Mark 5

IMPERIAL · METRIC	AMERICAN
8 oz./225 g. butter	1 cup butter
8 oz./225 g. sugar	1 cup sugar
5 eggs	5 eggs
8 oz./225 g. plain flour	2 cups all-purpose flour
4 oz./100 g. blanched almonds, coarsely chopped	1 cup coarsely chopped blanched almonds
4 oz./100 g. seeded raisins, chopped	scant 1 cup chopped seeded raisins

Beat the butter and sugar until soft and creamy. Add the eggs one at a time and beat thoroughly. Fold in the flour gradually. Grease a large roasting tin and sprinkle with flour. Spread the mixture in the tin. Sprinkle with the chopped almonds and raisins.

Bake on the centre shelf of a moderately hot oven for 30–40 minutes. Cut into small diamond shapes with a sharp knife while still warm. Cool on a wire tray and store in an airtight tin.

SEMOLINA CAKE IN SYRUP
(HALVAS TIS RINAS – GREECE)

Cooking time: 1 hour 10 minutes
Oven temperature: 350°F., 180°C., Gas Mark 4

Serves 4–6

IMPERIAL · METRIC	AMERICAN
6 oz./175 g. butter	$\frac{3}{4}$ cup butter
6 oz./175 g. castor sugar	$\frac{3}{4}$ cup sugar
$\frac{1}{2}$ teaspoon almond essence or grated rind of an orange	$\frac{1}{2}$ teaspoon almond extract or grated rind of an orange
3 eggs	3 eggs
9 oz./250 g. fine semolina	$1\frac{1}{2}$ cups fine semolina flour
3 oz./75 g. ground almonds	scant 1 cup ground almonds
1 level teaspoon baking powder	1 level teaspoon baking powder
1 oz./25 g. split blanched almonds	$\frac{1}{4}$ cup split blanched almonds
3 tablespoons brandy, wine or orange juice	scant $\frac{1}{4}$ cup brandy, wine or orange juice
Syrup:	**Syrup:**
4 oz./100 g. sugar	$\frac{1}{2}$ cup sugar
$\frac{1}{4}$ pint/1$\frac{1}{2}$ dl. water	$\frac{2}{3}$ cup water
1 tablespoon lemon juice	1 tablespoon lemon juice
2 tablespoons brandy, wine or orange juice	3 tablespoons brandy, wine or orange juice

Cream the butter, sugar, essence or orange rind. Beat in the eggs, one at a time. Stir in the sifted semolina, ground almonds and baking powder, then stir in the almonds and liquid. Turn into a well buttered 7-inch (18-cm.) cake tin. Bake in a moderate oven.

Make the syrup, meanwhile, by boiling the sugar and water until the syrup will form a thread between two spoons. Remove from the heat and add the lemon juice and brandy, wine or orange juice. Pour this hot syrup over the hot cake.

BAKED STRAWBERRY CAKE

(MANSIKKATORTTU – FINLAND)

Cooking time: 25–30 minutes
Oven temperature: 375°F., 190°C.,
Gas Mark 5

Serves 4

IMPERIAL · METRIC	AMERICAN
4 egg yolks	4 egg yolks
2 oz./50 g. castor sugar	$\frac{1}{4}$ cup sugar
2 oz./50 g. fine soft breadcrumbs	1 cup fine soft bread crumbs
1 teaspoon vanilla essence	1 teaspoon vanilla extract
1 16-oz./450-g. can strawberries	1 16-oz. can strawberries
4 egg whites	4 egg whites
whipped cream	whipped cream

Beat the egg yolks and sugar together until fluffy. Add the fine bread-crumbs, vanilla essence and half the drained strawberries. Fold in the stiffly whipped egg whites. Pour the mixture into a greased pie dish, about 2-pint (1-litre, 5-cup) size. Bake in the centre of a moderate oven for approximately 30 minutes. Decorate with the remainder of the strawberries and whipped cream. Serve hot or cold.

SWEET PASTRY

(MÜRBETEIG – GERMANY)

Cooking time: 35–40 minutes
Oven temperature: 375°F., 190°C.,
Gas Mark 5

IMPERIAL · METRIC	AMERICAN
2 oz./50 g. castor sugar	$\frac{1}{4}$ cup sugar
8 oz./225 g. plain flour	2 cups all-purpose flour
6 oz./175 g. butter	$\frac{3}{4}$ cup butter
1 egg	1 egg
1 tablespoon water	1 tablespoon water
1 16-oz./450-g. can sliced peaches	1 16-oz. can sliced peaches
1 oz./25 g. nuts, chopped	$\frac{1}{4}$ cup chopped nuts

Mix the sugar and flour, rub in the butter and mix to a firm dough with the egg and water. Roll out $\frac{1}{4}$ inch (0·5 cm.) thick, place on a lightly greased baking sheet. Cover with drained peaches.
  Bake in the oven. Serve hot or cold sprinkled with chopped nuts.

CHERRY FLAN

(LIMBURGSE VLAAI - HOLLAND)

Cooking time: 30 minutes
Oven temperature: 375°F., 190°C.,
Gas Mark 5

Serves 8

IMPERIAL · METRIC	AMERICAN
4 oz./100 g. butter	$\frac{1}{2}$ cup butter
6 oz./175 g. plain flour	$1\frac{1}{2}$ cups all-purpose flour
2 oz./50 g. castor sugar	$\frac{1}{4}$ cup sugar
1 egg yolk	1 egg yolk
1 medium can Morello cherries	1 medium can Morello cherries
1 heaped teaspoon arrowroot	1 heaped teaspoon arrowroot
$\frac{1}{4}$ pint/$1\frac{1}{2}$ dl. cherry juice	$\frac{2}{3}$ cup cherry juice
$\frac{1}{2}$ pint/3 dl. double cream	$1\frac{1}{4}$ cups whipping cream

Rub the butter into the flour until the mixture resembles breadcrumbs. Add the sugar, bind together with the egg yolk, and press into a well buttered 10-inch (26-cm.) flan or cake tin.
  Prick the bottom with a fork. Bake in the centre of a moderately hot oven for 30 minutes. Leave for 10 minutes to cool slightly before removing from the tin. Drain and stone the cherries and place on the pastry base. Make a glaze by blending the arrowroot with the cherry juice and heat until it thickens. Allow to cool slightly before spooning it over the cherries. Decorate with fresh whipped cream.

CHERRY GÂTEAU

(SCHWARZWÄLDER KIRSCHTORTE
– GERMANY)

Cooking time: 50–55 minutes
Oven temperature: 350°F., 180°C.,
Gas Mark 4

IMPERIAL · METRIC	AMERICAN
8 egg yolks	8 egg yolks
8 oz./225 g. castor sugar	1 cup sugar
2 oz./50 g. ground almonds	½ cup ground almonds
4 oz./115 g. plain flour	1 cup all-purpose flour
2 oz./50 g. cocoa powder*	½ cup unsweetened cocoa powder*
8 egg whites, stiffly beaten	8 egg whites, stiffly beaten
½ pint/3 dl. Kirsch	1¼ cups Kirsch
cherry jam	cherry jam or jelly
about ¼ pint/1½ dl. double cream	about ⅔ cup whipping cream
1 lb./½ kg. stoned cherries	1 lb. pitted cherries
2 oz./50 g. chocolate, grated	2 squares chocolate, grated
1 oz./25 g. icing sugar	¼ cup confectioners' sugar

Beat together the egg yolks and sugar until light and creamy. Fold in the ground almonds, flour, cocoa powder then egg whites. Put into a greased and floured cake tin, 8–9 inches (20–23 cm.) in diameter, and bake in a moderate oven for 50–55 minutes. When cool cut into three layers, soak in Kirsch. Spread the first layer with cherry jam. Spread the second layer with Kirsch flavoured cream and add the whole cherries. Cover with the third layer. Cover the whole gâteau with the rest of the cream. Cover the sides and top with grated chocolate and dust lightly with icing sugar. Eat the same day.

*Blended with 2 tablespoons boiling water and cooled. Or use 2 oz. (50 g.) melted chocolate instead.

PEACH SPONGE CAKE

(PESCHE RIPIENE – ITALY)

No cooking

Serves 4

IMPERIAL · METRIC	AMERICAN
1 block of sponge cake	1 block of plain cake
4 oz./100 g. hot raspberry jam, sieved	scant ½ cup sieved hot raspberry jam or jelly
2 oz./50 g. almonds, chopped	½ cup chopped almonds
cake or biscuit crumbs	cake or cookie crumbs
2 peaches	2 peaches
2 oz./50 g. ground almonds	½ cup ground almonds
2 tablespoons castor sugar	3 tablespoons sugar
sweet wine or Strega liqueur	sweet wine or Strega liqueur
4 almonds	4 almonds
jam sauce (see recipe)	jam sauce (see recipe)

Cut four rounds of sponge cake, about ¼ inch (0·5 cm.) thick, with a fancy cutter. Spread with half the jam, roll in chopped almonds and crumbs. Place on a plate and put half a peach on each round.
Mix together the ground almonds, sugar and most of the wine or liqueur. Spoon the mixture into an icing bag and fill the halved peaches. Put a whole blanched almond in the centre of each. Pour a jam sauce over (sieve remaining jam, thin with water and flavour with wine or liqueur).

BISCUITS, TWISTED INTO KNOTS OR BOWS

(ZELLER KRINGEL – SWITZERLAND)

Cooking time: 10 minutes
Oven temperature: 350°F., 180°C., Gas Mark 4

Makes about 30

IMPERIAL · METRIC	AMERICAN
1 hard-boiled egg	1 hard-cooked egg
3 oz./75 g. butter	6 tablespoons butter
4 oz./100 g. castor sugar	½ cup sugar
4 oz./100 g. plain flour	1 cup all-purpose flour
1 oz./25 g. Emmenthal or Gruyère cheese, grated	¼ cup grated Emmenthal or Gruyère cheese

Sieve the hard-boiled egg. Cream the butter and 3 oz. (75 g., 6 tablespoons) of the sugar together and add the sieved egg. Mix in the flour and grated cheese to make a dough. Chill for 30 minutes until the dough is firm. Roll out to ¼ inch (0·5 cm.) thick. Cut into strips 5–6 inches (13–15 cm.) long and form into shapes. Place on a greased baking tin. Sprinkle with the rest of the sugar.

Bake on the second shelf down in a moderate oven for 10 minutes until a light biscuit colour. Cool on a wire rack.

CROISSANTS

(FRANCE)
Illustrated in colour on page 57

Cooking time: 10–15 minutes
Oven temperature: 425°F., 220°C., Gas Mark 7

IMPERIAL · METRIC	AMERICAN
1 oz./25 g. fresh yeast	1 cake compressed yeast
1 oz./25 g. butter	2 tablespoons butter
2 teaspoons salt	2 teaspoons salt
1½ tablespoons sugar	2 tablespoons sugar
¼ pint/1½ dl. warm milk	⅔ cup warm milk
12 oz./350 g. flour	3 cups all-purpose flour
4 oz./100 g. butter	½ cup butter
1 egg yolk	1 egg yolk
milk	milk

Dissolve the yeast in a little warm water. Put the 1 oz. (25 g.) butter into a bowl with the salt and sugar and pour over the milk to melt the fat. Leave to cool to lukewarm, then add the dissolved yeast. Gradually add the flour to give a soft smooth dough. Cover the bowl with a damp cloth and leave for 2 hours. Knead the dough and put into a cold place to chill thoroughly, then roll it out on a floured board into a rectangle. Form the butter into a square and spread it evenly over the dough. Fold over the dough and roll out to a rectangle, then fold and roll again. Chill once more then roll and fold twice more at intervals of 30 minutes. Roll the dough out to ¼-inch (0·5-cm.) thickness and cut into 4-inch (10-cm.) squares. Divide each square into 2 triangles; roll up each triangle, starting at the longest base and rolling towards the point. Form into crescents and put on a lightly floured baking sheet. Beat the egg yolk with the milk and brush over the croissants. Bake for 10–15 minutes in a hot oven.

Salad dressings, sauces and miscellaneous

Salad dressings

VINAIGRETTE DRESSING

For salads and cold
vegetables

IMPERIAL · METRIC
1 rounded teaspoon finely chopped
   onion
good shake salt and pepper
¼ level teaspoon dry mustard
3 tablespoons salad oil
1 tablespoon tarragon vinegar

AMERICAN
1 rounded teaspoon finely chopped
   onion
good shake salt and pepper
¼ level teaspoon dry mustard
scant ¼ cup salad oil
1 tablespoon tarragon vinegar

Combine all the ingredients, place in a screw top jar. Shake until the ingredients emulsify. Allow to stand for 10 minutes before use.

MAYONNAISE

IMPERIAL · METRIC
2 egg yolks
½ teaspoon French mustard
½ teaspoon salt
½ teaspoon sugar
shake pepper
shake cayenne pepper
2 teaspoons lemon juice
½ pint/3 dl. best olive oil
2–3 tablespoons white wine vinegar

AMERICAN
2 egg yolks
½ teaspoon French mustard
½ teaspoon salt
½ teaspoon sugar
shake pepper
shake cayenne pepper
2 teaspoons lemon juice
1¼ cups best olive oil
3–4 tablespoons white wine vinegar

Put the egg yolks into a bowl. Add the mustard, salt, sugar, peppers and lemon juice. Whisk for 2 minutes. Drop in the olive oil gradually, whisking very well until about 2 tablespoons (U.S. 3 tablespoons) are added. Add a teaspoon of vinegar. Continue adding the oil. Add more vinegar if the sauce becomes too thick. The finished mayonnaise should be thick enough to show a spoon mark.

FRENCH DRESSING

For salads

IMPERIAL · METRIC
3 parts olive oil
1 part white wine vinegar
½ teaspoon salt
½ teaspoon pepper
chopped herbs, various mustards,
   garlic, mint, etc., may be added
   to taste

AMERICAN
3 parts olive oil
1 part white wine vinegar
½ teaspoon salt
½ teaspoon pepper
chopped herbs, various mustards,
   garlic, mint, etc., may be added
   to taste

Put the oil, seasoning and herbs (or mustard, etc.) into a small bowl – or into the salad bowl. Drop in the vinegar and beat well.

Sauces

BÉCHAMEL SAUCE

IMPERIAL · METRIC	AMERICAN
2 oz./50 g. butter	$\frac{1}{4}$ cup butter
2 oz./50 g. flour	$\frac{1}{2}$ cup all-purpose flour
1 pint/6 dl. milk	$2\frac{1}{2}$ cups milk
flavouring as required	flavoring as required

Melt the butter in a saucepan without colouring. Add the flour and cook over a low heat, stirring with a wooden spoon for a few minutes only. Remove from the heat. Add the milk slowly, stirring with each addition until smoothly blended. Return to the heat and stir until the sauce boils; cook, stirring continuously, for 2–3 minutes. Season, or sweeten, as liked.

For a thinner sauce, use $1\frac{1}{2}$ oz. (40 g., 3 tablespoons) butter and $1\frac{1}{2}$ oz. (40 g., 6 tablespoons) flour with the same amount of liquid.

Sauce Mornay – cheese sauce
To 1 pint (6 dl., $2\frac{1}{2}$ cups) of the sauce add $\frac{1}{2}$ teaspoon salt, a pinch of pepper and $\frac{1}{4}$ teaspoon dry mustard. After the sauce is cooked, stir in 4–6 oz. (100–175 g., 1–$1\frac{1}{2}$ cups) finely grated cheese.

Vanilla sauce
To 1 pint (6 dl., $2\frac{1}{2}$ cups) sauce add 1 tablespoon sugar and a few drops vanilla essence. Serve with steamed puddings and other puddings needing a sauce.

Cream sauce
For fish, poultry, eggs and vegetables.
Add $\frac{1}{4}$ pint ($1\frac{1}{2}$ dl., $\frac{2}{3}$ cup) fresh cream to 1 pint (6 dl., $2\frac{1}{2}$ cups) béchamel sauce and bring to boiling point. Add a few drops of lemon juice.

SAUCE TARTARE
For fried fish and grills

IMPERIAL · METRIC	AMERICAN
2 hard-boiled eggs	2 hard-cooked eggs
2 raw egg yolks	2 raw egg yolks
$\frac{1}{2}$ pint/3 dl. olive oil	$1\frac{1}{4}$ cups olive oil
1 tablespoon white vinegar	1 tablespoon white vinegar
salt and pepper	salt and pepper
1 teaspoon capers	1 teaspoon capers
1 teaspoon chopped gherkins	1 teaspoon chopped sweet dill pickle
1 teaspoon chopped herbs	1 teaspoon chopped herbs
3 tablespoons cream	scant $\frac{1}{4}$ cup cream

Sieve the two hard-boiled egg yolks into a basin. Stir in the two raw egg yolks. Drop in oil little by little. Add the vinegar when thickened. Season. Add the capers, gherkins, herbs, one chopped egg white and the cream.

QUICK TOMATO SAUCE

Cooking time: 10 minutes

IMPERIAL · METRIC
1 10½-oz./275-g. can condensed
    tomato soup
1 level tablespoon dry mustard
1 teaspoon sugar
1 tablespoon vinegar
6 tablespoons top of the milk or
    single cream

AMERICAN
1 10½-oz. can condensed tomato
    soup
1 level tablespoon dry mustard
1 teaspoon sugar
1 tablespoon vinegar
½ cup coffee cream

Bring the soup slowly to the boil, stirring all the time. Blend the mustard, sugar, vinegar and top of the milk and stir into the soup. Reheat without boiling.

Miscellaneous

ALMOND PASTE

For gâteaux, petits fours, etc.

IMPERIAL · METRIC
8 oz./225 g. ground almonds
8 oz./225 g. icing sugar or icing
    and castor sugar mixed

juice of ½ lemon
1 teaspoon almond essence
1 teaspoon vanilla essence or
    1 teaspoon maraschino
about 2 egg whites

AMERICAN
2 cups ground almonds
1¾ cups confectioners' sugar or
    confectioners' sugar and sugar
    mixed
juice of ½ lemon
1 teaspoon almond extract
1 teaspoon vanilla extract or
    1 teaspoon maraschino
about 2 egg whites

Mix all the ingredients except the egg whites. Add sufficient lightly whisked egg white to bind to a firm consistency. Knead lightly and roll out on a sugared board.

GLACÉ ICING

Icing to coat large or small cakes

IMPERIAL · METRIC
8 oz./225 g. icing sugar
2 tablespoons warm water
flavouring and colouring

AMERICAN
about 1¾ cups confectioners' sugar
3 tablespoons warm water
flavoring and coloring

Sieve the icing sugar. Add the water, stir until smooth and consistency to coat the back of a spoon. Flavour and colour, then pour over the cake at once and leave to set.

BUTTER CREAM

For filling cakes

IMPERIAL · METRIC
3 oz./75 g. butter
3–4 oz./75–100 g. icing sugar
½ tablespoon cold milk
½ tablespoon hot water
vanilla essence or other colour
    and flavour as liked

AMERICAN
6 tablespoons butter
¾–1 cup confectioners' sugar
½ tablespoon cold milk
½ tablespoon hot water
vanilla extract or other color and
    flavor as liked

Cream the butter well and gradually beat in the icing sugar. Continue beating until very smooth and white, then beat in the milk and water. Add the colouring and flavouring as liked.

COFFEE SYRUP FLAVOURING

Use as a delicious flavouring for cakes, biscuits, icings, desserts and ices

Cooking time: 3 minutes

IMPERIAL · METRIC	AMERICAN
1 pint/6 dl. boiling water	2½ cups boiling water
6 oz./175 g. ground coffee	scant 2 cups ground coffee
½ teaspoon vanilla essence	½ teaspoon vanilla extract
6 oz./175 g. lump or granulated sugar	¾ cup lump or granulated sugar

Pour the boiling water over the coffee in a pan, stir well over the heat for 1 minute. Leave until cold, then strain through muslin. Stir in the vanilla essence and the sugar. Return to the heat, stirring well, for 2 minutes. Cool, pour into a bottle and seal.

CRÈME CHANTILLY

Whipped cream – to serve with desserts

Serves 8

IMPERIAL · METRIC	AMERICAN
1 pint/6 dl. double cream	2½ cups whipping cream
1 oz./25 g. icing sugar, sweetened with vanilla pod or ½ teaspoon vanilla essence	¼ cup confectioners' sugar, sweetened with vanilla bean or ½ teaspoon vanilla extract
1 egg white	1 egg white

Whip the cream in a bowl until beginning to thicken. Fold in the sifted icing sugar and vanilla essence. Whisk the egg white until stiff and then fold into the cream very carefully. Turn into a glass bowl.

COFFEE WITH BRANDY
(CAFÉ BRÛLÉ)

Makes 4 large cups

IMPERIAL · METRIC	AMERICAN
¼ pint/1½ dl. brandy	⅔ cup brandy
6 lumps sugar	6 lumps sugar
rind of 1 lemon	rind of 1 lemon
2 sticks cinnamon	2 sticks cinnamon
1 pint/6 dl. hot, strong black coffee	2½ cups hot, strong black coffee

Put the brandy, sugar, lemon rind and cinnamon in a chafing dish or saucepan and bring to the boil. Remove from the heat and set light to it. When the flames die down, add the coffee and serve immediately.

Index